THE GENIUS WHEEL

HARNESS THE POWER OF YOUR 7-YEAR PERSONAL GROWTH CYCLE

LULU MINNS

Edited by
MARY-ROSE LOBO

Illustrated by
CARA MINNS JOHNSON

Copyright © 2025 by Lulu Minns

Illustrations © 2025 by Cara Minns Johnson

All rights reserved.

No part of this book may be reproduced in any form or by any electronic or mechanical means, including information storage and retrieval systems, without written permission from the author, except for the use of brief quotations in a book review.

For permissions requests, contact:

Lulu Minns: lulu@thegeniuswheel.com

Cara Minns-Johnson: carajohnson973@gmail.com

ISBN: **978-1-83709-123-2**

First edition, 2025

Published by Lulu Minns

West, 2, 5 Rock Pl, Kemptown, Brighton and Hove, Brighton BN2 1PF

The Genius Wheel®

Introduction

Part I: Understanding Genius

Chapter 1 – What is Genius?
Chapter 2 – When is my Genius Phase?
Chapter 3 – The Evolution of Jennifer Aniston's Genius

Part II: Understanding the Cycle

Chapter 4 – The Polarity Principle
Chapter 5 – Why are Cycles Misunderstood?
Chapter 6 – The Seasonal Cycle (12-month cycle)
Chapter 7 – Your Macro Cycle (7-year cycle)
Chapter 8 – Your Micro Cycle (29.5-day cycle)
Chapter 9 – The Power of Ritual
Chapter 10 – Using your Genius Wheel

WHAT OTHER WOMEN HAVE SAID ABOUT HARNESSING THE POWER OF THEIR 7-YEAR CYCLE

I'm now able to plot where I might be within the cycles and an awareness of each of the different seasons' challenges and benefits. And it gave me the clarity and confidence to move forward. — Faye

The 7-year growth cycle has opened my thoughts/memories to aspects of my life that will change my future! Lulu is able to delve in a way that gets to the essence of you and the work will not only benefit you but all of those around you. — Louise

When I reflected on the last 7 years I really saw a pattern in what's been happening and I've been exploring. It made me feel hopeful, rather than quite lost and a bit bewildered. — Cat

The 7-year cycle gave me so much to think about, but no pressure to get to answers or to fit someone else's agenda. — Catherine

I found it so fascinating looking back over my last couple of cycles. I realised I separated from my husband in the month, I turned 35 so as I entered my 5th cycle! — Jacqui

Wow, a penny drop moment when I reflected on my 7-year cycle in this way. — *Emma*

Drawing out the significant events from the last 7 years and noticing the patterns in my behaviour, responses and experiences is really important data! I'm using this to evolve my own business and leadership. — *Kat*

Focusing on my 7-year cycle has really been a transformative experience. — *Clare*

I can now understand and utilise my power in each cycle, helping me move through them with more focus and intention . — *Claire*

DEDICATION

For both of my Grandmothers, Joan a talented writer and Alice, a talented pianist.

THE GENIUS WHEEL: HARNESS THE POWER OF YOUR 7-YEAR PERSONAL GROWTH CYCLE

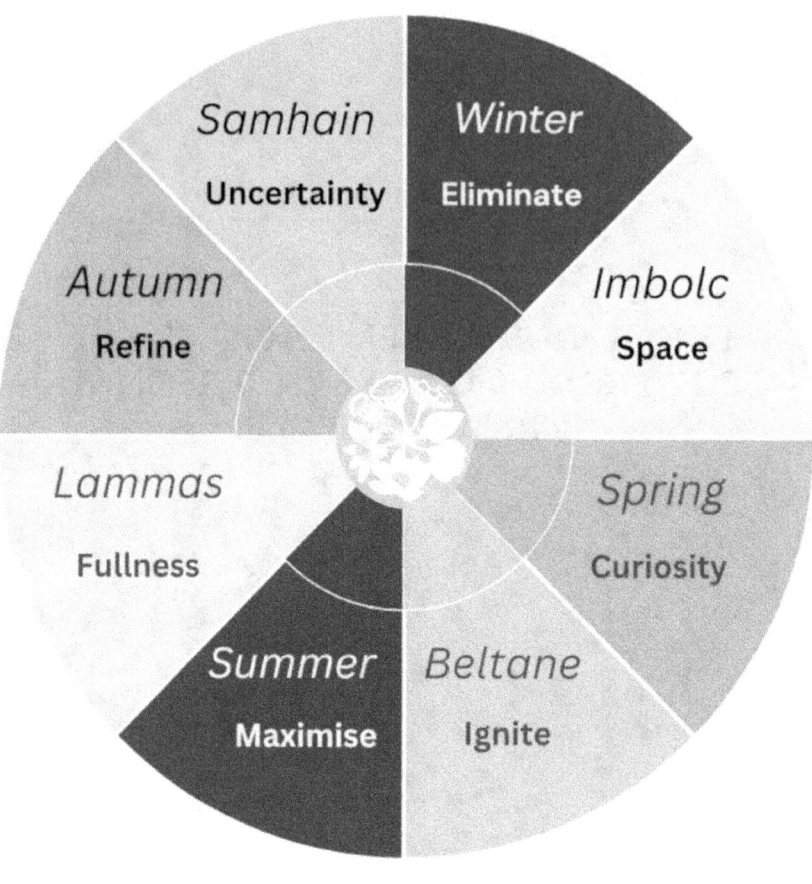

INTRODUCTION

Before The Genius Wheel® presented itself to me, I found myself deep in reflection, untangling the cycles and patterns that had shaped my personal and professional journey. It was during this time of introspection that I made a bold, transformative decision: to channel everything I had learned into creating the most impactful coaching programme of my career.

This wasn't just about creating something for the sake of it — it was about supporting transformation. First and foremost, for my clients, then as a creator, for myself. And ultimately, for the future of my business, which I had struggled with during the UK lockdowns of 2020–2021, a time when I, like many of us, felt adrift and unmotivated.

It was a powerful intention — a spark that would reignite not just my work, but my purpose. Little did I know, The Genius Wheel® would become the cornerstone of that vision.

When I launched my first coaching programme for women leaders in 2016, I knew I was creating something truly unique — something that couldn't be found in a textbook, a weekend course, or executive leadership programme. This wasn't coaching by the numbers; it was something much deeper.

Fast forward to 2024, during one of my retreats, a client perfectly captured what makes my work stand out. She said, "There is something so special about what you do. It's grounded, it's safe, and it's authentic. And because of that, it allows us — the women you support — to embody those qualities too."

Her words affirmed what I've always known. My work is rooted in more than just skill — it's a culmination of a lifelong study of human behaviour and gender dynamics, a passion I've been immersed in since I was 16. Everything I teach is infused with feminine principles and a deep respect for evolution, creating a space where women can truly thrive, unapologetically and authentically.

Sometimes, my clients struggled to articulate the profound impact our work together had on their lives. They knew it was transformative but couldn't always find the words to describe it. What they *did* know — and loved — was that my approach was anything but prescribed. I met them exactly where they were, 1000%, tailoring everything to their unique needs. While this worked wonders for my clients, it created a major challenge for me: how could I market something so intuitive and personalised? What specific problem was I solving, and why?

I sought advice from numerous coaches and marketers, but no one could quite pinpoint the essence of what I did — or how I did it.

When working with me, clients experienced shifts both personally and professionally. Without even realising it, I had been intuitively meeting them within their own personal development cycles. I could sense when it was time for them to pull back and reflect or, conversely, when they were ready to step boldly forward. It was an innate ability, not easily boxed into marketing buzzwords, but it was the key to the lasting impact I had on the people I worked with.

"Contraction is the key to expansion," I'd remind my clients time and time again. This simple yet powerful truth became the lynchpin of our work together. Much like my days as a practising lawyer, my relationships with clients often extended far beyond a brief 3-month coaching engagement. They kept coming back, and our connection deepened over time.

Clients would share reflections like, "Whenever I see you, I find my way back to my path," or, "You're the only coach who can get me back on track with where I'm meant to be." These words affirmed the unique role I played in their journey — not just as a guide, but as someone who helped them tune into their inner rhythm.

If they were in a phase of contraction, they'd exhale with relief, finally granting themselves the permission to pause, reflect and step back. If it was time for expansion, they'd charge forward with newfound clarity and confidence, ready to embrace their next leap. Each phase — whether pulling inward or boldly stepping outward — was met with exactly what they needed to realign and thrive in the moment.

I firmly believe that there is no one-size-fits-all blueprint for success. True genius isn't something we find outside ourselves — it's something we cultivate from within. Yet in today's world, drowning in oversharing and an overwhelming flood of information, it's all too easy to fall into the trap of searching for a guru, a formula or a strategic model that promises to deliver results based on *their* journey.

The truth is, the most transformative work happens when you tap into your own inner wisdom. That's the focus of this book and the way I coach intuitively: helping you unlock and leverage the power of your unique 7-year personal growth cycle. This process isn't about following someone else's roadmap — it's about uncovering the one that's already been gifted to you.

When you look inward, rather than outward, you create something far more powerful and sustainable. It's not about replicating someone else's journey — it's about carving your own path, one that aligns with your evolution, and empowers you to thrive on your own terms.

Every woman's personal growth journey unfolds in unique 7-year cycles, each revealing the brilliance and potential she has to offer the world. Embracing your individual growth plan, aligning with your energy, and understanding where you stand in life are essential to thriving. Ignoring your personal challenges and opportunities — or trying to mimic someone else's path — only makes the journey more difficult.

In today's age of social media and constant information overload, it's all too easy to get swept up in comparison and distraction, losing sight of your own unique gifts and inner wisdom. But true growth comes from tuning into yourself, honouring your challenges, and unlocking the distinct opportunities that are uniquely yours to explore and embrace.

Unlike many in the coaching industry, I embrace the interplay of fate and free will, recognising that not everything in life can or should be controlled. Fate — what some may call destiny or *'written in the stars'*, represents the forces beyond our grasp. Learning to distinguish between what we can influence and what we cannot is a profound act of self-awareness and empowerment. To suggest we hold complete control over every aspect of our lives, businesses, or careers is unrealistic. What we *can* control, however, is our response. When we view the uncontrollable as part of our personal growth cycle, it unlocks a deeper sense of purpose and resilience.

Certain aspects of life such as when, where and to whom we are born, are beyond human choice. These factors, along with the conditions of our childhood, often shape both our genius and the hidden barriers that hold us back. Similarly, events like global pandemics, illnesses in loved ones, and other uncontrollable forces impact how we move forward. Timing, too, often exists outside our sphere of influence. Embracing these truths doesn't limit us — it empowers us to grow in harmony with life's rhythms rather than constantly pushing against them.

Growth, whether in business, creativity, or life isn't always something we can rush or force. It unfolds in cycles of contraction and expansion, and the magic lies in trusting the process. By aligning with this natural rhythm, we open ourselves to innovation, transformation and the fullest expression of our genius.

The creation of The Genius Wheel® epitomised this philosophy for me. Though simple in concept for me to write, the process was anything but linear. Developing transformational coaching programmes had always come naturally since I began my business 7 years earlier. But The Genius Wheel® was different — it was a whole growth cycle in the making. I knew it would be powerful, but I had to trust its timing. I stopped, started, created and discarded along the way. At times, I felt myself forcing progress instead of allowing it to flow. It wasn't until I surrendered to the process — allowing both contraction and expansion — that The Genius Wheel® truly came to life. Trusting my personal growth cycle was essential, and in doing so, I created something unique and transformative on a completely new level.

Before the pandemic in 2019, I launched She Rebel Radio®, a podcast celebrated for its counter-status quo ideas and unapologetic infusion of feminine perspective. Organically, the podcast grew to over 20,000 downloads, attracting sponsorships for our renowned International Women's Day series. It's been described as a platform that challenges convention while offering a fresh and dynamic lens through which women can view their own leadership, creativity and growth.

From the end of 2021 to June 2023 — while I patiently waited and sometimes tried to push — I also thought about quitting the business several times over, but my regular clients kept asking for coaching, She Rebel Radio® was doing well and the retreats I hosted were well received. My work as always was deepening but I'd turned 40, and felt slightly bored in my professional and personal life —I wanted something even deeper.

A close friend commented that she'd noticed the depths of my despair around my 40th birthday and didn't know how to help me. She was grateful that she knew I was well resourced to work my way through it, as she herself didn't know how to help. I, on the other hand, had thought I'd done quite well covering it up!

I began to reflect and noticed that 7 years prior, I'd been in a very similar energy as a criminal defence lawyer and litigator who thought about quitting for nearly two years before I eventually did. That was in December 2014 and in December 2021, 7 years later, I went into the new year in a similar place. Not feeling sure about my business, my relationships choices over the past cycle, and not being sure about where I wanted to be living for the foreseeable future. I was in a space of everything and nothing being wrong, all at the same time.

'Bury me under a rock and leave me' in 2028, I thought as this 7-year cycle I'd heard about was definitely a thing. In 2007, I'd qualified as a lawyer and moved from London back to my home town of Brighton. In 2000, I left Brighton and went to university in Manchester — and similarly in 1993, I was aged 12, and there was so much happening for me — I was doing all sorts of things I shouldn't have been doing as I shifted from innocence into adolescence!

What I didn't know was that in all those moments of my life, *I was in my macro season of WINTER*. There was a clear ending and a clear beginning of the next phase. And the cycle began again.

Winter occurs in our 7-year cycle at least once and I'm sorry to break it to you, it lasts for approximately 21 months. *Winter* is characterised by the energy of uncertainty and elimination but whatever happens in our *winter phase* **always** informs the next phase of growth and direction. And we must remember what always follows *winter* is SPRING!

The Genius Wheel® has 8 distinct phases and by using these you can chart your course through your own 7-year personal growth cycle. There are fluctuations within each cycle and by using the seasons we can begin to predict and feel into the energy of each phase — this book will give you the tools to do that.

Who is this book for?

This book is for those who are ready to break free from the noise of the modern world — the endless blueprints, quick fixes and "proven" strategies that promise success but fail to honour the individuality of your journey. It's for those who know, deep down, that their path to growth and fulfilment can't be found in someone else's formula.

If you've ever felt overwhelmed by the constant flood of advice, or frustrated by the pressure to follow systems that don't resonate, this book is your guide. It's for the person who knows their potential is waiting to be unlocked — not by looking outward for answers, but by turning inward to discover the wisdom, cycles and genius already within them.

Whether you're navigating personal growth, craving professional alignment or seeking clarity on your next step, this book is for you. It's for those who understand that real transformation isn't about copying someone else's journey but about uncovering the unique rhythm of your own.

This is for the seekers, the dreamers, and the creators who are ready to embrace their inner authority, honour their personal evolution, and chart a path that feels authentic, powerful and entirely their own. If you're ready to reclaim your genius and trust your process, this book will show you how.

You might have picked up this book because you sense a chapter of your life is closing, or perhaps an exciting new beginning is just on the horizon. Maybe you're feeling uncertain about what needs to change or unsure of how to take the next step. Or perhaps you're standing at a crossroads, overwhelmed yet excited by where you are, both personally and professionally, seeking the tools to navigate your next chapter with clarity, wisdom and intention. Whatever has brought you here, this book will guide you through all the phases of your 7-year personal growth cycle, equipping you with insights to embrace change and move forward consciously.

You'll discover how to harness the unique energy of the season you're in whist preparing for the challenges and opportunities of seasons yet to come. You'll learn to chart a clear path forward and uncover valuable lessons from your past that may have been overlooked — empowering you to grow with purpose and intention.

This is a guide for women committed to their personal growth. Women who know there's always a higher level of their brilliance waiting to emerge. It's for those who want to see more women in control of their genius, thriving in their authenticity, and shaping a world where their voices and talents lead the way. As Dolly Parton wisely said, "Our job is to find out who we are and do it on purpose." Your 7-year personal growth cycle is a powerful tool to help you do just that.

In 1928, Virginia Woolf combined two essays to create *A Room of One's Own*, a groundbreaking work in which she challenged us to imagine a future — 100 years on — where women and their genius could truly thrive. Whilst progress has undeniably been made, we've also witnessed setbacks, particularly in the wake of the 2020 pandemic, which saw the global women's movement lose ground in critical ways.

Now, as we approach the centenary of Woolf's vision in 2028, we must ask ourselves: would she be impressed by the strides we've made, or disheartened — like so many of us — by how much still hasn't changed?

How can we bring greater conscious awareness to our lives, breaking free from the cycles that keep us stuck in work and roles that don't ignite our passion? And how do we ensure that the next generation of girls and women don't inherit the same battles, repeating a cycle we've already fought to break? Woolf's question is as urgent now as it was then: what must we do to create a world where women's genius can truly flourish?

Let's imagine a world with more peace, harmony and balance — a world where women have the tools *and the time* to meet their genius. This book is written on the premise that while we as women are equal, we are also inherently different. It's a call to embrace our feminine nature, using it as a source of power and wisdom to guide our personal growth and unlock the genius within. Together, we'll uncover how to move through life with intention and grace, in alignment with who we truly are.

What to expect

Personal growth encompasses every facet of our evolution and wellbeing — spiritual, emotional, mental, physical, social and even financial. When we thrive in our personal growth, we gain a deeper understanding of ourselves and what we need to unlock our highest potential. The 21st century is a pivotal era for women — one where reaching new heights in entrepreneurship and leadership is redefining what's possible.

The way I guide women through this process is two-fold. Firstly, we focus on the emotional and inner work — often issues that have been ignored for years suddenly demand attention, refusing to let us move forward into the next phase of our lives, businesses or careers. This critical work typically happens during the 'spiritual' or macro cycle of *winter*, although it can begin in late *autumn* and extend into early *spring*. Once this foundational work is complete, the focus shifts outward — towards how they're impacting the world. This phase of outward expression usually aligns with the macro cycle of *summer* but often begins in late *spring* and carries into early *autumn*. *Autumn* and *spring* are transitional phases, bridging the inner and outer work in a seamless, natural order. You'll discover more about this fascinating seasonal cycle in Chapter 6.

The 7-year personal growth cycle — rooted in the heroine's journey, as opposed to the hero's journey — remains an underexplored narrative. The concept is missing from mainstream thinking not only because the number 7 itself is mysterious and non-linear, but also because cycles, and the cyclical nature of all things, are inherently feminine. Rudolf Steiner is one of the few names associated with this concept, yet its absence from the mainstream highlights the broader tendency to overlook the power of feminine frameworks. The 7-year cycle offers profound insights for women ready to embrace their cyclical nature and step fully into their power.

Life and business rarely unfold in a straight line. When we embrace the reality that both our personal and professional lives move through cycles, we unlock the potential for greater wisdom, growth, and maturity with each new phase. As humans, we are here to evolve — not to remain stuck in the same old patterns of behaviour and mistakes. Yet, time and again, we see these patterns playing out in our own lives and on the world stage, where leaders, devoid of fresh ideas, continue recycling outdated solutions.

In today's information age, we are bombarded with endless blueprints, agendas, and advice from others on how to 'live better'. This overload of external input can disconnect us from our own instincts and personal growth cycles. It's all too easy to get swept up in what others think we should or shouldn't be doing, chasing promised solutions or rigid plans that may not align with our unique paths. For anyone who has ever started a business, the sheer volume of advice and frameworks can be overwhelming. How do you discern what's right for you, or when it's the right time to act?

This is where understanding your personal growth cycle, and using tools like The Genius Wheel®, becomes transformative. The Genius Wheel® acts as a filter for decision-making, helping you tune into your own cycle and bring more of your innate wisdom and maturity to every choice. It empowers you to stay aligned with your own rhythm, rather than chasing external agendas.

With The Genius Wheel®, we can also shift our perspective on so-called missed opportunities. Cycles remind us that opportunities are never truly lost — they come back around in their own time. This understanding encourages us to face what's holding us back, break through the blocks, and elevate our awareness. By embracing the cyclical nature of life, we not only navigate challenges with greater ease but also bring deeper consciousness to every stage of our journey.

In today's unpredictable world, where systems and organisations often falter, the wisdom of cycles and seasons offers a powerful tool for navigating what's next. Despite the chaos in the wider picture, aligning with your personal growth cycle provides a sense of safety, security and the reassuring knowledge that *this too shall pass*.

As women, we carry so much for others — holding, supporting and nurturing those around us. The Genius Wheel® brings a profound relief in recognising that at all times, one of the seasons is holding *you*. Your growth is always cradled within the natural rhythm of the seasonal cycle. The more deeply you understand the phase you're in, the more grounded and supported you'll feel as you move through it.

Discovering your own rhythm within your personal growth cycle is a game-changer. It allows you to work fluidly with past, present and future versions of yourself, uncovering lessons you may have missed and gaining insights to prepare for the next phase. This cyclical approach shifts your understanding of time from a rigid, linear path to a dynamic, ever-evolving flow.

The Genius Wheel® becomes your guide and filter for decision-making. It helps you determine whether now is the time to step into a leadership role, pursue or release a relationship, hire a sales coach or embark on a new course. By tuning into your season and cycle, you can plan and predict with clarity and confidence, aligning your actions with the natural rhythms of your growth. With The Genius Wheel®, you'll navigate life with greater ease, intention, and self-awareness.

Personal growth isn't a straight path — it's a dynamic, cyclical journey that unfolds in recurring patterns, weaving the fabric of your unique experience and shaping your path forward. These cycles are often mysterious, yet they hold the key to understanding how your life has unfolded and where it's heading next.

Your 7-year personal growth cycle acts like a map, revealing the rhythms and patterns that have shaped your past and continue to influence your present. When you understand where you are within this cycle, you gain the clarity and insight needed to chart your course with intention and confidence. It's a tool for navigating your life's journey with purpose, aligning with your natural rhythms, and unlocking the potential that lies ahead.

REFLECTION:

Before we dive in, let's take a moment for intentional self-reflection to begin your journey with your unique 7-year personal growth cycle. This exercise will help you connect with the cyclical nature of your growth by comparing where you are now to where you were 7 years ago.

If you're reading this in 2025
— what did 2018 look like for you?
If you're reading this in 2026
— what did 2019 look like for you?
If you're reading this in 2027
— what did 2020 look like for you?

What were the themes of that time? What lessons, opportunities, or wins shaped your experience? How did those moments influence who you are today? As you reflect, notice the patterns and connections between then and now — these insights are the foundation of understanding your 7-year personal growth cycle.

There's no right or wrong way to approach this reflection. You don't need to know exactly what phase you're in just yet. Simply tune in to what comes up for you and trust the process — it's all part of your unique journey.

For me, in 2024, I found myself in the vibrant phase of *spring* — a season brimming with fresh energy and excitement for my work. 7 years prior to this, in 2017, I hosted my first retreat in Morocco and welcomed a wave of inspiring new clients, and launched my website at the end of the year. It felt like emerging from a challenging chapter into a brighter, more promising time.

In 2024, I felt that same sense of renewal and momentum. I hosted two sold-out retreats — culminations of years of dedication — and am diving much deeper into my work with clients. Writing this book has been a powerful new chapter, another milestone in my ongoing evolution.

You can find out more about me and my work at thegeniuswheel.com or why not join *The Genius Wheel*® community on Substack.[1] You'll receive a welcome pack full of resources to help you get even more from this book.

---

1. luluminns.substack.com

PART I
UNDERSTANDING GENIUS

1
WHAT IS GENIUS

Your Genius is a Convergence — A Coming Together of your Sacred Gifts

The word 'genius' is universally understood, yet elusive to define. We often reserve it for others, seldom claiming it for ourselves. Society tells us genius is rare, belonging only to the few. When we hear the word, we may instantly think of figures like Albert Einstein, Wolfgang Mozart or William Shakespeare — images often steeped in archetypes of older, white, male brilliance. Even though the concept of genius has been tied to the divine and our soul's purpose, historically it's seen as a masculine archetype, further distancing many women from identifying with it.

But genius isn't confined to those narrow stereotypes — it is dynamic, diverse and alive within all of us. The Genius Wheel® reclaims and redefines this imagery, offering a framework that reflects the cyclical, sacred, and inclusive nature of genius. It shifts the narrative from something external and unattainable to something deeply personal and present within you. Your genius doesn't need to look like anyone else's — it's yours to uncover, nurture, and embody in your own extraordinary way.

In the 1950s, psychologist Abraham Maslow introduced his *Hierarchy of Needs* model, which outlined the fundamental needs humans must fulfil to reach self-actualisation — the point where one's potential and purpose can fully unfold. He said: *"A musician must make music, an artist must paint, a poet must write, if he is to be at peace with himself. What a man can be, he must be. This is the need we may call self-actualisation referring to a person's desire for fulfilment, namely the tendency to actually become what we are potentially."* According to Maslow, our human needs progress from physiological essentials (water, food, shelter etc) to safety and security, then to love and belonging, and finally to self-esteem and prestige before self-actualisation can occur.

While Maslow's work brought valuable insights into human motivation, it also reinforced a deeply embedded bias: the idea that genius, and the pinnacle of human potential, belongs primarily to men. His model reflected a male-dominated perspective of success and fulfilment, inadvertently leaving out the cyclical, relational, and diverse ways in which women actualise their own genius.

It's time to challenge and expand this narrative, recognising that genius is not confined to a narrow archetype. Genius is fluid, multifaceted and present in everyone. It's not about outperforming others in one domain but about weaving together your unique talents, experiences and gifts into something profoundly meaningful and impactful.

In pre-modern times, creative expression was likely a universal part of life. People danced, played music, and created art to communicate and express their emotions, relying on somatic and heart-based awareness rather than the linear, mind-dominated approach of the modern world. Yet, for most women, advancing one's genius would have been nearly impossible. While scholars agree that genius is innate within us, they also acknowledge that it requires a degree of privilege to nurture and expand it — something historically denied to the majority, especially women.

We cannot advance our genius when we are consumed by survival, wondering where our next meal will come from or in searching for a safe place to use the toilet without fear of violence. Without meeting our basic physiological and safety needs, as outlined in Maslow's hierarchy of needs, the possibility of self-actualisation is out of reach — a harsh reality that still affects countless women worldwide.

Even if our fundamental needs are met, genius isn't something we can simply 'work hard' to achieve if we lack the inherent spark of talent or interest. Genius is not chosen or earned — it is gifted. It's a birthright, inherited through family lines and embedded in the essence of who we are. It represents our potentiality, the ability to become all that we are capable of but have not yet realised. Our role is to uncover it, and the framework of the 7-year personal growth cycle offers us a pathway to do so.

Since the rise of patriarchal societies, women have often been defined by their relationships to others — primarily as wives and mothers. This framing has limited women's access to self-actualisation, with Maslow himself suggesting that women could only reach their potential through their husbands and children, not for their own sake or via their own talent. His hierarchy of needs, which championed being all that we can be but are yet to be, was conceived primarily with men in mind.

"What dreams? Ladies do not have dreams. They have husbands."
Portia Featherington (Bridgerton)

Now is the time to challenge this outdated perspective. Women's genius is not tethered to others; it is ours to claim, explore and advance for ourselves. By recognising and embracing the cyclical nature of growth and using tools like the 7-year personal growth cycle, we can step into our full potential and redefine what it means to realise our genius.

In a *Room of One's Own*, Virginia Woolf invites us to imagine if Shakespeare had an equally gifted sister. How would her story have unfolded in a world that silenced women's potential? Woolf envisions a starkly different fate: Shakespeare's sister would have been denied an education, her genius stifled by the expectations of domestic life. Instead of honing her craft, she would have been told to 'mind the stew or mend the stockings' and pushed into an early marriage. Her brilliance, unrecognised and unsupported, would have been extinguished before it had the chance to shine.

And the truth is, we all know those women because they exist within our own families. As my maternal grandmother, Joan Davies, once wrote to my grandfather in 1945: *"You must get supremely bored with the trivial little things I drivel about when writing to you, while you are making history, living in suspense, doing brave deeds whilst I simply take the dog out and wash up..."*

I have many of her letters and she was a fantastic writer. My paternal grandmother was a talented pianist but denied the same education as her brother. Both of them fulfilled the expectation and requirement in becoming mothers and wives.

We must acknowledge the 'feminine tragedy'[1] of our grandmothers, many of our mothers and women such as Zelda Fitzgerald and Marianne Faithfull. Their talents, their words and cultural brilliance were often hidden behind their male counterparts. And within society, they were undervalued, under recognised and even diminished and demeaned.

Perhaps we need not simply imagine Shakesphere's sister, because Mozart had an equally talented sister called Anna Maria Mozart. From the age of 7, she played concerts all around the world with their father, Leopold. But once she reached the age of 18 (just half way

---

1. *Parachute Women* by Elizabeth Winder

though her 3rd personal growth cycle) she was sent back to Salzburg to be married. Whilst she continued to teach the piano to others, it was her younger brother Wolfgang who built his reputation and recognition as a musical genius. Letters between them appear to indicate she may have also written her own compositions. If she did, she'd never have been permitted to take the credit for her own work. It would not have been acceptable to outshine the men in her life.

"Publicity in women is detestable. Anonymity runs in their blood. The desire to be veiled still possesses them. They are not concerned about the health of their fame as men are and, speaking generally, will pass a tombstone or a signpost without feeling an irresistible desire to cut their names on it" — Virginia Woolf[2]

In Ancient Rome, the very worst thing a woman could do was *'to be talked about or bring attention to herself'*. It didn't matter if this was because she had *'accomplished something'* or had *'done something wrong'* — Natalie Haynes[3]

Instead of being celebrated for her talents, Anna Maria was expected — no, required — to live within the narrow roles of wife and mother. She lived to 78, which means the world was deprived of her brilliance for over 6 decades — or 8 personal growth cycles. That loss has always felt like a quiet call to action: a reminder to honour the women who came before us by refusing to dim our own light. So let's not hold back any longer. The world needs your gifts — now more than ever.

When we step into our unique genius — we feel fulfilled and stop comparing ourselves to others. When we step away from that unique genius — we feel the gap between us and 'it'. We may get frustrated at what others are doing or start comparing ourselves but this is a

---

2. *A Room of One's Own*, by Virginia Woolf
3. *Pandora's Jar,* Women in Greek Myths by Natalie Haynes

totally normal part of the process. It is a signifier to you, that you've been stepping away from or are not quite listening to 'the deeper call' of your genius.

To fully grasp this dynamic, it is helpful to explore the word 'genius' in both its most basic and ancient sense. You can also use the time to reflect on how your own genius may manifest itself.

The Basic Sense of Genius

Genius is more than an abstract concept — it is the manifestation of exceptional intelligence, creative power, or a natural ability. The following exercise invites you to explore and claim your unique genius. While genius may seem complex, breaking it down into these categories provides clarity and insight:

A. **Exceptional intelligence** — The ability to solve problems and generate innovative solutions.
B. **Creative power** — The capacity to bring forth original ideas and manifest them into reality.
C. **Natural ability** — A strong influence over others through presence, words, or actions.

Below we dive into 4 exercises for you to explore and claim parts of your genius :

1: Discovering Your Genius

Read the 3 categories above. Which one — **A, B, or C** — evokes the strongest reaction in you? Perhaps it stirs a sense of longing or recognition. Without overthinking, choose the category that resonates most with your unique genius.

Now, take a moment to reflect: Do you feel any resistance in identifying with one of these categories? Who came to mind with each category? Do you find yourself dismissing the possibility of possessing genius because you don't compare yourself to figures like Einstein (exceptional intelligence), Shakespeare (creative power), or Martin Luther King Jr. (natural ability)?

As women, we have often been conditioned to believe that genius belongs to a select few ... historically, mostly white men who had the privilege to cultivate their talents. But genius is not exclusive. It is within you, too. Togther, we can reframe this narrative:

- **Marie Curie** embodied exceptional intelligence.
- **Virginia Woolf** exemplified extraordinary creative power.
- **Oprah Winfrey** possesses a remarkable natural ability to inspire and connect.

When we expand our perception of genius to include women, it becomes easier to see ourselves within that frame. Remember: if we can't see it, we can't be it.

Now, be bold — choose the category that speaks to you the most.

2. Understanding your Legacy

If you could leave a legacy similar to one of the following individuals, who would it be? And why?

- **Albert Einstein or Marie Curie?**

- William Shakespeare or Virginia Woolf?
- Martin Luther King Jr. or Oprah Winfrey?

The choices we make here provide insight into our inherent genius and the power we hold within.

Recognising our genius can be challenging, especially when societal narratives have historically sidelined women in these spaces. This can result in us downplaying or dismissing our own brilliance. But genius is not confined to a privileged few — it is the unique fusion of our sacred gifts, nurtured under the right circumstances.

As Virginia Woolf famously said, *"A woman must have money and a room of her own if she is to write fiction."* This insight extends beyond writing — it highlights the fundamental need for space and resources to cultivate any form of genius.

If given the right circumstances, which aspect of your genius would you choose to cultivate? Exceptional intelligence, creative power or natural ability?

3. Claiming your Power

Now, take an active step in claiming your genius by completing this sentence:

I, (insert name), take active ambition of my (natural ability/creative power/exceptional intelligence) to (fill in your purpose or goal).

By stating this, you acknowledge your potential and commit to nurturing your unique genius.

Your genius is yours to embrace. How will you create the space to nurture and express it?

4. Creating the Space for your Genius

In *The Big Leap*, Gay Hendricks[4] introduces the concept of the 'zone

---

4. *The Big Leap*, Take Life to the Next Level by Gay Hendricks

of genius,' distinguishing it from the other zones of "non-competence," "competence" and "excellence." Hendricks highlights how so many of us become stuck in our zones of competence or excellence, rarely breaking through to our zone of genius. This reinforces the belief — or reality — that genius is reserved for only a select few.

As women, we must be especially mindful of what I call 'the curse of competence'. The more capable and talented we are, the easier it is to get trapped in doing *everything*, all the time. Social conditioning often places an unfair burden on women, expecting us to shoulder more than our fair share in both the workplace and the home. This relentless overextension not only leads to burnout but increases the likelihood of being stuck in mediocrity or confined to our zone of competence. Breaking free from this cycle is essential if we are to step fully into our genius and create lives of true purpose and impact.

In the book *Deep Work*, Cal Halrod[5] extends this principle and writes that in order for Carl Jung to unleash his genius into the world of psychiatry, he did 3 things:

1. Reduced his face to face client work (which meant periods of time with zero clients).
2. Ensured he had access to a retreat where he could work without being disturbed.
3. Had servants (and a wife) looking after him.

This enabled Jung to dive into the depth of his work and to create theories such as 'collective consciousness' which is a cornerstone of modern psychology. To undertake 'deep work' takes both time and space and a chance of being in wonder of the world to see the patterns of where your work could take you and what it is, you are really here to do.

---

5. *Deep Work*, Rules for Focused Success in a Distracted World by Cal Halrod

The idea that 'genius' is within everyone's reach remains a powerful yet underexploited truth. Many of us fail to fully unlock our potential, hindered by pervasive beliefs and societal constructs. We often hear, or infer from societal cues, that we're 'not good enough' and that genius is a rare trait reserved for a select few, predominantly men.

Moreover, societal structures further restrict us. The steep costs of living, an education system that prioritises conformity and traditional intelligence over creativity, and societal expectations for women[6] to prioritise others' needs over their own, all act as barriers.

We tend to settle within our 'zones of competence' or 'zones of excellence' — spaces where we feel safe and unchallenged. Venturing beyond these zones involves risks: the boldness required can attract rejection and criticism, which women face disproportionately. This fear of judgment reinforces the comfort of conformity and stifles the pursuit of true genius.

REFLECTION:
Take your journal and reflect honestly on where you might need to delegate more:

- Are you spending too much time minding the stew or mending the stockings when your time is best spent elsewhere?
- Are you trying to do everything yourself instead of delegating to others who might handle certain tasks more efficiently?
- Identify at least one task in your business that you could delegate — to a team member, freelancer or external support.
- Identify at least one household task you could delegate

---

6. *Invisible Women,* Exposing the Data Bias in a World Designed by Men by Caroline Criado-Perez

— to your children, partner or a hired professional such as a cleaner.

How might holding onto these tasks be distracting you from operating in your zone of genius? What impact would just an extra 15 minutes per day, dedicated solely to your genius, have on your work and life?

Write a list of tasks that fall within your zone of genius — those that only you can do. How can you shift more of your focus here?

By recognising what you can let go of, you free yourself to fully step into your brilliance.

So let's turn to exploring genius within its ancient sense, which further enables us to get to the grips of the magic our genius offers to each and every one of us.

The Ancient Sense

As identified above, In *The Big Leap*, Gay Hendricks introduces the concept of the 'zone of genius' — an area distinctly separate from other zones. This 'zone' is not just a space but a dynamic intersection where our unique strengths, skills and talents converge. It's at this very intersection that our genius takes form. While each of these attributes might not stand out individually, when they intertwine — BOOM! — that's where our unique genius or 'zone' emerges. This 'meeting point' of our personal threads is where our uniqueness is created, and what is more fascinating is these threads tend to run throughout the course of our entire lives. Which is why understanding your 7-year growth cycle can help you uncover them.

To explore genius in its ancient sense, we turn to the work of Irish poet and conversationalist David Whyte[7]. His words on this topic are profoundly compelling, and I deeply resonate with his perspective on

---

7. *Consolations, The Solace, Nourishment and Underlying Meaning of Everyday Words* by David Whyte

genius. While my own genius may not be poetic in nature, I consider meaningful conversations — ones that spark transformation and change — to be within my zone of genius. So, let's explore this concept together.

Whyte reminds us that the word *genius* originates from the Latin term *Genius Loci*, which refers to the 'prevailing character or atmosphere of a place' or 'the presiding god or spirit of that place'. In Ancient Rome, genius was considered not an individual trait but rather an energy connected to place and land. This historical perspective offers a fascinating contrast to our modern understanding, shifting the focus from personal brilliance to something more collective and environmental.

Whyte also invites us to consider that the ancient meaning of *Genius Loci* holds the key to understanding the genius within ourselves. If the genius of a place is its 'prevailing character, atmosphere, or presiding god or spirit,' then by extension, our personal genius is our own 'prevailing character, atmosphere or inner guiding spirit'.

This challenges the conventional belief — deeply rooted in many religious traditions — that divinity is separate from us, existing outside rather than within. Historically, God has been depicted as a solitary figure of masculinity, a notion I have personally struggled with and rejected. This perspective is particularly striking given my own lineage: My mother comes from a strong line of Protestant priests. While she was baptised in accordance with family tradition, my grandfather later broke away from this legacy and was not religious himself.

As such, I grew up rejecting all things religious, even upsetting a primary school teacher for saying: *"My mum and dad made me — not God,"* and looking back I was deeply frustrated by the lack of female narrative within the stories of religion and creation. Conversely, whilst my absolute rejection of religion continued to prevail in secondary school, as a compulsory subject it was something I excelled at. And sometimes, I wonder if that is due to the family lineage.

The notion of God or Spirit can be deeply personal and, for many, even triggering — shaped by our lineage, culture and gender. For the purpose of this book 'god, spirit, or energy' represents the field of intelligence and consciousness to which we all belong. This field is composed of both masculine and feminine energy, which we will explore further in Part II.

Returning to the ancient concept — genius invites us to recognise and access the genius within ourselves — 'our prevailing character, atmosphere, god or spirit within'. Let's acknowledge that each of us carries a unique spirit, an individual atmosphere that surrounds us. Energy, by nature, cannot be destroyed. The real question is: How can we fully embrace this essence of ourselves? And more importantly, how can we intentionally harness its power to shape our lives and impact the world around us?

Our Genius is a Conversation

Within the ancient sense, our genius is not a fixed destination but an ongoing conversation. By observing the cycles of life and engaging in dialogue with the world around us — whether through nature, people or ideas — we can begin to uncover the genius within ourselves.

Every conversation we've ever had, every moment of connection, every decision we've made has led us to where we are now. These interactions — both internal and external — form the landscape of our unfolding genius. Conversations are not just words; they are movements, energetic exchanges of ideas, observations and insights. Through them, we inherit wisdom, shape our perspectives, and contribute our unique imprint to the world.

Like constellations in the night sky, each of us forms a pattern that is distinct and irreplaceable. Just as no two stars align in exactly the same way, no two people share the same genius. We are like fractals — complex, ever-evolving, yet inherently patterned. Our uniqueness is our strength.

Thumbprint by Eve Merriam

In the heel of my thumb
    are whorls, whirls, wheels
    in a unique design:
    mine alone.
    What a treasure to own!
    My own flesh, my own feelings.
    No other, however grand or base,
    can ever contain the same.
    My signature,
    thumbing the pages of my time.
    My universe key,
    my singularity.
    Impress, implant,
    I am myself
    of all my atom parts I am the sum.
    And out of my blood and my brain
    I make my own interior weather,
    my own sun and rain.
    Imprint my mark upon the world,
    whatever I shall become.

Instead of seeking genius as an external achievement, embrace it as an ongoing conversation — an evolving dance of ideas, relationships, and self-discovery. Trust that your unique imprint is unfolding exactly as it should and that your 7-year personal growth cycle can help you to converse with it.

REFLECTION:

Head over to The Genius Wheel® Substack[8] to download the genius constellation meditation and once you've listened to it, record your 3 sacred gifts below.

Note these may be images, feelings, colours or something not tangible but simply write down what comes up. Remember part of the conversation with your genius is by sharing what comes up even when it's not perfect or fully understood. This is all part of the conversation.

Gift 1:

Gift 2:

Gift 3:

---

8. luluminns.substack.com

2
WHEN IS MY GENIUS PHASE?

Recognising our genius is only the first step — understanding *when* to harness its full power is just as important. The answer lies within our *genius phase*, which unfolds during our **7th (age 42), 8th (age 49), and 9th (age 56) personal growth cycles.** These are the pivotal years when our genius becomes most accessible, potent and ready to be fully expressed.

It is here that we reach a unique meeting point within ourselves, where our sacred gifts come together. This can feel profoundly overwhelming, as it often coincides with the transition into menopause — a time when society is most inclined to disregard us as women.

In the early 20th century, philosopher Rudolph Steiner spoke extensively about human development in 7-year cycles, linking them to astrological and spiritual influences. He stated that our 7th cycle (ages 42 to 49) was guided by Saturn (the 7th planet) helping individuals develop self-mastery and deep wisdom. This phase is about moving from ambition (and external validation) to meaningful contribution. He said our 8th cycle (49 to 56) was ruled by the Moon (as is our 1st personal growth cycle), but this time at a higher octave emphasising spiritual integration and reflection on our life's journey — particularly, I would add, as to work we are here to do. The 9th cycle (56 to 63) he said was ruled by Mercury, the planet of communication but at a higher octave (having been present in our 2nd personal growth cycle aged 7 to 14) and this phase is typically marked by deeper inner understanding and desire to share knowledge with others.

Whilst I do not reject his model, I do not include the ruling of each phase by any particular planet but rather integrate the seasonal cycle within each of the 7-year cycles and simply call the 7th, 8th and 9th personal growth cycle — your genius phase.

It's important to note that harnessing the power of your 7-year personal growth cycle is not meant to speed up or manipulate the process of meeting our genius. Rather, it is about *recognising the cyclical nature of our journey* — bringing deeper awareness to ourselves, our wisdom, and our maturity as we move through each growth cycle. It helps us to keep moving and not stay stuck. With this awareness, we can more easily see and navigate our genius phase, understanding that each 7-year cycle serves as preparation for the next phase.

Instead of feeling worn down by life's challenges or believing we've missed opportunities or made too many mistakes, we can cultivate **trust in our unique paths**. No matter how many twists and turns we take, we will eventually arrive at a profound meeting point within ourselves — a place where our experiences, insights and purpose align in a way that is uniquely our own.

. . .

WICCAN AND PAGAN traditions **recognised and honoured** the *Triple Goddess*, represented through 3 female archetypes: **the Maiden, the Mother, and the Crone.** Each of these corresponds with a distinct stage in a woman's life cycle and aligns with the 3 primary phases of the moon. The **Maiden** (waxing moon) symbolises youth growth, and new beginnings — representing the phase *before* children. This can also represent the season of spring and element of air. The **Mother** (full moon) embodies creation, nurturing and fulfillment—representing the phase *during* motherhood. This can also represent the season of summer and element of fire. The **Crone** (waning or dark moon) represents wisdom, reflection and transformation — symbolising the phase *after* children. This can also represent the season of winter and the element of earth[1].

Image A

---

[1]. *Wild Magical Soul,* Untame your Spirit and Connect to Natures Wisdom by Monica Crosson

. . .

THE TRIPLE GODDESS simplifies our existence to child bearers and the *autumn phase is missing* — and with it, the element of *water*. **The autumn phase is our genius phase and is the most vital and transformative stage of all.** Paired with the element of water, this phase embodies flow, deep wisdom and intuition — just as water carves through rock over time, lived experience shapes our purpose and legacy. Spiritual and emotional fulfillment take priority, along with a deeper connection to ourselves and those ready for more meaningful conversations.

THIS PERSPECTIVE EXPANDS our understanding of **purpose, contribution and identity** beyond our ability to have children. It acknowledges that a woman's legacy extends far beyond motherhood — and it doesn't matter whether we have children or not. It's important to **reclaim this phase** as a time of profound creativity, wisdom and impact. It is a time of **refinement, harvest and transition** — the moment when all of our experiences, wisdom, and talents converge. **It is the culmination of our genius.**

"OUR CULTURE HAS PREVIOUSLY ATTEMPTED to exclude women who are no longer needing a mate or to bear children, there has been, if not fear, then certainly suspicion of such women. But rather than allowing this vital phase to be erased, we must ask: How can we harness this energy? Now that our focus shifts, how can we channel our wisdom and power to create meaningful change in the world?"
   Sharon Blackie [2]

. . .

---

2. *Hagitude*, Reimagining the Second Half of Life by Sharon Blackie (plus She Rebel Radio® episode) https://sites.libsyn.com/210074/if-women-rose-rooted-with-sharon-blackie

WE CAN ALSO DESCRIBE this phase as our **golden era** — a time of deep transformation, where we may feel a desire for recklessness, an internal explosion, or 'even a complete reorganisation of our psyche'.[3] It is also a phase rich with full-circle moments. However, unlike the earlier preparation phases of our lives, where we may have been more impulsive or externally driven, this stage is marked by a deeper sense of **responsibility**. We are no longer selfish but rather self-full — honouring our own needs while also considering our impact on the world.

A POWERFUL EXAMPLE of this kind of growth is **Tracey Emin**. In 2024, at the age of 60 (her 9th personal growth cycle) she was honoured with a damehood for her lifetime contribution to art. Her work was first recognised in 1997 at the start of her 6th personal growth cycle (35–42) — it was raw, unapologetic, and deeply personal. In 1999 she was nominated for the *Turner Prize*, solidifying her place as a major female figure in contemporary art. Then, in 2020, life took a harrowing turn as she was diagnosed with terminal cancer. But rather than retreat, she revived her creative practice with renewed urgency and depth. She went on to found the *Tracey Emin Foundation* and the *Tracey Emin Artist Residency Programme* — initiatives that now support emerging artists in her hometown of Margate. Her journey is a testament not only to resilience, but to the ever-evolving nature of genius.

EMIN'S DAMEHOOD is a beautiful coming home — a full-circle moment both in her work and in returning to where she grew up. Her art remains just as relevant today as it was in the 1990s, but now, her legacy carries even greater weight. Reflecting on her damehood,

---

3. *Wise Power* by Alexandra Pope and Sjanie Wurlitzer (plus She Rebel Radio® episode) https://sites.libsyn.com/210074/my-wise-power-with-alexandra-pope-and-sjanie

Emin remarked[4], "*It gives me a louder voice to do the things that I think are important.*"

AND WITH THAT she has always been a voice for women in respect of trauma and their place in the art world.

EMIN'S JOURNEY is a clear example of how our earlier preparation phases — where we first establish our creative voice — can mirror into our *autumn*/genius phase, where we bring our wisdom, influence and power to new heights.

IN PART II of the book, we will connect more fully to the seasonal shifts that occur within each 7 years. By making the time to stop, we continue the conversation with our genius and excavate the gifts that are buried for us.

"THE UNIVERSE BURIES *strange jewels deep within us all, and stands back to see if we can find them*"
    Elizabeth Gilbert [5]

REFLECTION:
I've created 2 resources, the first includes the genius phase within our life cycle as it's important that we do not allow this vital phase to be erased.

Within this framework, I work with 4 archetypes: the Maiden, the Go-Getter, the Genius, and the Wise Woman. Each archetype corre-

---

4. https://www.whitecube.com/news/tracey-emin-honoured-with-damehood
5. *Big Magic,* Creative Living Beyond Fear by Elizabeth Gilbert

to a moon phase, an element, a season, a cardinal direction, and a phase of the fertility cycle.

BY DOING SO, I aim to honour us all as women and our shared life phases. The term 'Go-Getter' is intended to be inclusive of women as mothers, business go-getters and those who choose or experience both — either way, it is our busiest phase.

So let's dive in.

1. **The Life Cycle**

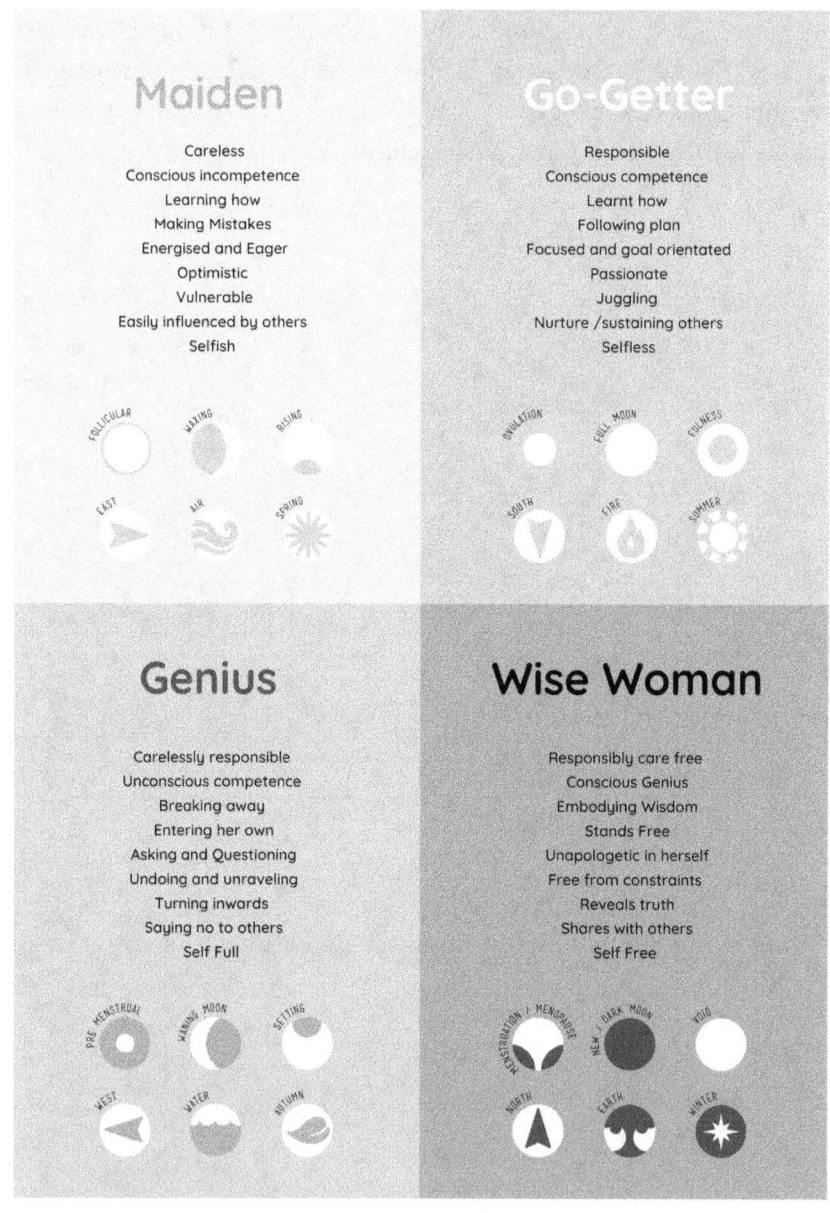

2. Secondly, you can identify your cycle on the next page. If your age falls within 2 brackets, you are transitioning from one phase to the next. Select the phase ahead of you.

Age	Cycle	Phase
0 to 7	1st Personal Growth Cycle	Growing up
7 to 14	2nd Personal Growth Cycle	Growing up
14 to 21	3rd Personal Growth Cycle	Growing up
21 to 28	4th Personal Growth Cycle	1st Prep phase
28 to 35	5th Personal Growth Cycle	2nd Prep phase
35 to 42	6th Personal Growth Cycle	3rd Prep phase
42 to 49	7th Personal Growth Cycle	Genius phase
49 to 56	8th Personal Growth Cycle	Genius phase
56 to 63	9th Personal Growth Cycle	Genius phase
63 to 70	10th Personal Growth Cycle	Consolidation phase
70 to 77	11th Personal Growth Cycle	Reflection phase
77 to 84	12th Personal Growth Cycle	Reflection phase
84 to 91	13th Personal Growth Cycle	Reflection phase
91 to 98	14th Personal Growth Cycle	Bonus phase

Within The Genius Wheel® Substack[6] community you can download your 7-year timeline and colour PDFs outlining the 4 phases of our life cycle. You can also connect with me via thegeniuswheel.com or lulu@thegeniuswheel.com.

---

6. luluminns.substack.com

3

THE EVOLUTION OF JENNIFER ANISTON'S GENIUS

To illustrate how our genius culminates, I want to share the brilliance of Jennifer Aniston and how her genius has evolved through her 8 previous personal growth cycles. In February 2025, Jen turned 56 and entered her 9th personal growth cycle.

LAUNCHED to stardom (1991–1996)

Jennifer Aniston's rise to fame began in 1994 when she stepped into her iconic role as Rachel Green in *Friends*. The show became one of the most-watched sitcoms of all time, propelling her career to incredible heights, with the cast eventually earning £1 million per episode. At 25, she was halfway through her 4th personal growth cycle, which is the 1st of 3 preparation phases and foundational. At the start of this cycle, aged 21, she had secured her first recurring television role in *Molloy*, and in 1993, she made her feature film debut in *Leprechaun*. Both television and film would go on to define her career. By 1996, as her 4th cycle neared its end, she won a Screen Actors Guild Award (SAG) for her performance in *Friends*.

. . .

Fame (1997–2003)

Aniston's stardom continued throughout her 5th personal growth cycle (ages 28–35). She remained dedicated to *Friends* throughout this 7-year period, further solidifying her place on screen. In 1998, she began dating Brad Pitt, and together, they became one of the most sought-after power couples in Hollywood. They married in 2000, positioning themselves to maximise the potential of both their relationship and their careers. Between 2002 and 2003, Aniston won both an Emmy Award and a Golden Globe. However, despite her outward success, she was experiencing an internal shift. She was eager to explore new acting opportunities and was hesitant about returning for the 10th season of *Friends*. Ultimately, she became the cast member most eager to move on and embrace new challenges.

A catalyst for change (2004–2010)

In May 2004, the final episode of *Friends* aired, marking the beginning of Aniston's transition into her 6th personal growth cycle at age 35. Just months later, in early 2005, she announced her separation from Brad Pitt amidst speculation about his relationship with *Mr and Mrs Smith* co-star Angelina Jolie. Later that year, their divorce was finalised. During this period, she embraced the rom-com phase of her film career and dated her *The Break-Up* co-star Vince Vaughn, whom she credited with bringing her back to life. This phase served as a preparation period for her career reinvention, as she gradually distanced herself from her *Friends* persona and established herself as a leading actress in Hollywood. However, it was clear that many of her roles still echoed elements of Rachel Green.

Finding courage and confidence (2011–2017)

At 42, Aniston entered her genius phase, a time of confidence, risk-taking, and creative expansion. She embarked on a long-term relationship with Justin Theroux and took on unexpected roles, including her portrayal of a bold, Cruella De Vil-type character in

Horrible Bosses. This daring departure from her usual roles earned her the award for Best On-Screen Dirtbag — an accolade few could have imagined for the actress best known as Rachel or the quintessential rom-com girl next door.

She further demonstrated her evolving artistry by starring in and executively producing *Cake*, a critically acclaimed drama that earned her the Best Actress award at the Independent Film Festival and a Golden Globe nomination. A few years later, she married Justin Theroux, marking another personal milestone.

INDEPENDENCE AND SHOWCASING **growth (2018–2024)**

As Aniston entered her 8th personal growth cycle at 49, she divorced Justin Theroux. Unlike after her first marriage, this time she chose not to rush into another relationship, instead embracing personal growth and self-discovery. She also opened up about her fertility struggles in her late 30s and early 40s, a topic that resonated with many women facing similar challenges.

IN 2019, *The Morning Show* premiered, with Aniston as both the lead character and executive producer. In her role as Alex Levy, she explored sexism in the television industry and the ethical dilemmas of career advancement. This project highlighted her growth as an executive producer, a skill she had been refining during her previous cycles. With a reported salary of £2 million per episode, she won her second SAG Award for an outstanding performance. This moment marked a full-circle achievement, cementing her legacy beyond just acting. Given Hollywood's history of sidelining women over 35, her continued success is particularly significant.

BUT THAT WASN'T ALL. In 2021, she launched her own haircare brand, a project she had been developing for years. Given her longstanding association with iconic hairstyles — especially "The Rachel" from *Friends* — this venture felt like another full-circle moment. She reflected on her journey, saying,[1]

"I FEEL the best in who I am today, better than I ever did in my 20s or 30s even, or my mid-40s. We need to stop saying bad things to ourselves. You're going to be 65 one day and think, 'I looked fantastic at 53.'"

. . .

---

1. tps://www.independent.co.uk/life-style/jennifer-aniston-social-media-allure-b2221602.html

MOST RECENTLY, *The Morning Show* aired its 4th season, and Aniston has actively promoted Pvolve, a Pilates-based fitness brand. Her ability to stay relevant and adapt to evolving trends continues to inspire many, particularly women over 50.

REFLECTION:

What might Jennifer Aniston's personal growth cycle reveal about your own? How can understanding these phases help you recognise the patterns shaping your choices and achievements?

TAKE a moment to reflect on your journey. How have your personal growth cycles influenced your biggest decisions, challenges and breakthroughs?

TO EXPLORE THIS FURTHER, join me on Substack[2] for more celebrity case studies, and download the 7-year timeline PDF to map out your own path.

THEN, I invite you to go one step further — write your own personal growth story using the 7-year cycles as markers. You may be surprised by the insights you uncover.

AND THAT BRINGS us to the next chapter — where things get even more exciting.

IN **PART II**, you'll meet **Jo Myles**, our real-life case study for this book. Of course, Jennifer Aniston is a real person too, but I don't

---

2. luluminns.substack.com

exactly have her on speed dial! Jo is also living proof of just how powerful and transformative your **7-year personal growth cycle** can be.

Here's the incredible part — I wrote about her journey without ever speaking to her, yet she resonated with every word. That's how precise and universal your 7-year personal growth cycle is. Refer to **Appendix A** (after the Acknowledgments section at the end of the book), for the full case study.

Are you ready to see it in action? Let's dive in.

PART II

UNDERSTANDING THE CYCLE

4

THE POLARITY PRINCIPLE

Two Opposing but Complementary Forces Where One Cannot Exist Without the Other

Before we begin, as promised I'd love for you to meet Jo Myles, our case study for Part II of the book — refer to **Appendix A** (after the Acknowledgments section at the end of the book), for the full case study. I first saw Jo speaking at a *Thrive*[1] event hosted by entrepreneurship educator and expert, Clare Griffiths in Brighton. As she spoke, I was struck by her openness — she shared her personal and professional journey with remarkable honesty — but what stood out even more was how clearly I could hear the 7-year shifts within her story.

JO'S JOURNEY honours both the contractions and expansions of our

---

1. Thrive is on a mission to boost the number of female-led small businesses https://www.thriveinbusiness.co.uk/our-founder

personal growth, including her earlier cycles of working with Alexander McQueen, having children, starting her incredibly successful *Not On The High Street* business called *3 Blonde Bears* (named after her children) as well as a scary and life-shifting cancer diagnosis. When Jo and I spoke and she agreed to share her story in this book, she reflected on how, as women, we may be able to separate our personal and professional lives — but often, we simply don't want to. This is a premise that I coach and run retreats upon. Separation is often a masculine principle, while wholeness — or the ability to embrace all aspects of life at any one time — is a feminine one. We need both of these principles in balance to survive, which is where the polarity principle comes in.

THE POLARITY PRINCIPLE is based on the idea that the universe we live in is built on polar opposites. Everything exists in contrast — light and dark, expansion and contraction, masculine and feminine. *Two opposing but complementary forces where one cannot exist without the other.* They are opposites but two sides of the same coin.

POLARITY IS fundamental in the sciences. In chemistry, it refers to the study of chemical bonds and the interactions between molecules. In the social sciences, polarity can be seen in opposing perspectives, particularly in political views which in recent years, we've witnessed an increasing amount of, often to extreme levels.

MY FAVOURITE WAY TO understand polarity is by thinking about a TV remote control. We've all put the batteries in the wrong way at some point, only to realise they need to be positioned opposite to one another for the device to work and for electricity to flow. The same principle applies to us when it comes to accessing our masculine and feminine energy. These two forces may seem opposite, but they are complementary — one cannot exist or function fully without the other. When balanced, they create a natural flow, just like the energy within a working remote.

IN NATURE, birth cannot occur without the meeting of two opposing forces. This is a universal truth. The same principle applies when we birth ideas, creations and manifestations. When we learn to balance both our masculine and feminine energies, we experience a greater sense of flow, alignment, and ease in bringing our visions to life.

IT'S important to recognise that we all carry masculine and feminine energy regardless of gender. These two energies are meant to act in harmony with one another but when they fall out of balance, our natural flow and rhythm in life become disrupted. We find ourselves caught up in maintaining one extreme [2] of energy whilst struggling to integrate the other.

MORE OFTEN THAN NOT, masculine energy dominates feminine energy. Society has conditioned us to value masculine traits — such as logic, productivity, and control — over the feminine qualities of intuition, creativity and receptivity. As a result, many of us have become disconnected from our feminine energy, leading to burnout, stress and exhaustion.

THIS IMBALANCE DOESN'T JUST AFFECT us individually — it plays out on a global scale, where we see excessive force, conflict and disharmony. To restore balance, both within ourselves and in the world, we must learn to reconnect with and honour both energies.

---

[2]. *Untethered Soul: T*he Journey Beyond Yourself by Michael A Singer

PART of the process of awakening the feminine energy within ourselves is to rediscover the cyclical nature living inside each and every one of us. Feminine energy is cyclical in nature whereas masculine energy is more of a straight or linear line. The straight line and the circle are polar opposites — yet one cannot exist without the other.

IF WE CONSIDER the straight line to represent masculine energy — it is linear, structured, consistent and certain. In contrast, a circle embodies feminine energy — it is cyclical, fluid, rhythmic and mysterious. Both are essential. When we learn to embrace both in our lives, we create a natural balance between structure and flow, certainty and change. If, like me, you chose a corporate career — such as training to be a lawyer, doctor or vet — you would have followed a linear path to reach your goal. Consistency was key. There was a clear starting point, middle and end, with each step building logically on the last.

THE LINEAR or the straight line is a sequence of events or thought processes that logically lead from one to the other. There is no interruption or significant deviation from this linear line. This is the nature of masculine energy — structured, goal-oriented, and progressive. In contrast, the feminine energy follows a more cyclical, fluid path, one that embraces detours, intuition, and evolution rather than a fixed destination. The circular path was hugely respected in the ancient and Celtic world.

"THE CELTIC MIND was never drawn to the single line; it avoided ways of seeing or being which seek satisfaction in certainty. The celtic mind had a wonderful respect for the mystery of the circle and the spiral. The circle is one of the oldest and most powerful symbols. The world is a circle. So is the sun and the moon."

John O'Donaguhe[3]

OUR ANCESTORS once believed the world was flat, not circular. To me, this mirrors the way we often view life — as linear, rather than recognising the power of cycles. Personal growth is typically seen as a straight line — a journey with a clear before and after, always moving upward towards a goal. But in reality, growth is cyclical. We experience patterns, phases and seasons, often revisiting lessons in deeper ways rather than simply moving in a straight path forward.

BY EMBRACING THIS CYCLICAL NATURE, we can navigate change with more ease, awareness and flow. Rather than resisting repetitive or mysterious patterns, we can learn to move with their natural rhythm. We begin to understand that life is made up of periods of contraction and expansion. We may even find ourselves returning to the starting point, not as a failure, but as part of our continuous cycle. Instead of a straight path, growth follows a repeating pattern, with natural fluctuations of energy and evolution. A perfect example of this is the stock market, which rises and falls in cycles — just like our 7-year personal growth cycle.

THE CYCLICAL IS INHERENTLY FEMININE. Nature itself reflects this rhythm — the moon and tides move in cycles, as do our menstrual cycles. The seasons follow a predictable, repeating pattern, each one flowing into the next. Throughout this book, you'll notice that I call this the *seasonal promise*. By recognising these natural cycles, we can use one to inform the other — a concept we'll explore further with The Genius Wheel® framework.

---

3. *Anam Cara,* Spiritual Wisdom from the Celtic World by John O'Donaghue

"Even time itself has a circular nature, the day and the year are built into a circle. At its most intimate level so is the life of each individual."
  John O Donaghue[4]

Our bodies have a circadian rhythm or 'body clock' which is a natural or internal process that governs the sleep-wake cycle and repeats roughly every 24 hours. There are many things in the modern world that disrupt our natural circadian rhythm such as jet lag, work shifts, caffeine, alcohol and even the white light from our technological devices. When my circadian rhythm is in sync, I'm most alert workwise in the mornings and I naturally feel sleepy around 3 p.m. and 10 p.m. — like clockwork. Because it is clockwork — a biological rhythm governed by nature itself. We can think of our 7-year personal growth cycle as our energetic clock — one that, when we tune into it, allows us to work with our cycles rather than against them.

In today's linear world, we are conditioned to focus on end destinations and constant, measurable growth. As a result, the circular — with its perceived unpredictable, rhythmic nature — is often dismissed as something to be controlled or overlooked. This mirrors how women and their cycles have historically been treated. A key example of this is in medical research, a traditionally male-dominated field. As such, much of the medical field's early testing was conducted on men, excluding women due to the fluctuations of our menstrual cycle. Rather than recognising these natural variations, researchers deemed them too inconsistent, too complex, and too difficult to measure. During menstruation and the perimenopause, our hormones and body temperature fluctuate — as is the nature of a cycle. Yet instead of working with this rhythm, science largely ignored it. The result? The masculine, linear model became the dominant framework — the so-called universal 'truth'.

---

4. *Anam Cara*, Spiritual Wisdom from the Celtic World by John O'Donaghue

. . .

BUT THIS IS A MISTRUTH, where we all feel the consequences — whether in healthcare, the climate, business or beyond. It's time to reclaim the wisdom of the *cyclical* and recognise the power it holds.

WHAT DOES this mean for your 7-year personal growth cycle?

- There is no end destination — your personal growth cycle is continuous.
- Like an energetic clock, your energy will fluctuate throughout the cycle.
- Patterns will repeat, allowing you to predict and work with your natural rhythms.
- Your personal growth cycle is unique, bringing its own challenges and opportunities.
- Cycles seek completeness, often bringing you full-circle moments — where you return to the origin's source, position, or situation, but with a transformed perspective.

DEMI MOORE EXPERIENCED a powerful full-circle moment when she finally won a Golden Globe, after nearly hitting the mark in 1991, 1993, and 1994. During her 4th personal growth cycle (ages 28 to 35), she earned nominations but didn't win the award for *Ghost*, *Indecent Proposal* or *Disclosure*.

DESPITE HER CONTINUING SUCCESS, she was often dismissed as a 'popcorn actress', struggling to gain full critical recognition.

. . .

At 62, during her 9th personal growth cycle (ages 56 to 63), she finally won a Golden Globe and received the acclaim she truly deserved for *The Substance*. In her acceptance speech, she reflected on the low moments of her career, proving that growth is never a straight line — it is cyclical, filled with doubt, reinvention, and eventual recognition.

Her journey reminds us that our own personal cycles bring us back to familiar places — but with newfound wisdom, strength, and perspective.

Ambika Mod also described this beautifully in a podcast interview with Josh Smith[5], where she reflected on visiting Arthur's Seat in Edinburgh during the Fringe Festival. At the time, she was questioning whether pursuing an acting career was truly worth it.

3 years later, she returned to Arthur's Seat — but this time, as the lead in the Netflix smash hit *One Day*. That very career she had once doubted has propelled her to household-name status. This is the essence of a full-circle moment — standing in the same place, yet seeing it from a completely different perspective.

As we'll explore in Chapter 7, it's likely that Ambika was in her *winter* phase on her first visit to Arthur's Seat — facing doubt and introspection — whilst post filming (3 years later, half of the cycle), she had stepped into her *summer* phase, a time of visibility, expansion, and success.

. . .

---

5. https://podcasts.apple.com/us/podcast/ep-109-ambika-mod/id1549676420?i=1000645129932

REFLECTION:

Think back to a time when you found yourself in a familiar place, situation, or experience, but with a completely different mindset, perspective, or role. This could be in your career, relationships, personal growth or a specific life event.

1. **The starting point:** Can you recall a moment when you questioned something important in your life — your path, career, relationships, or purpose? Where were you physically, emotionally or mentally at that time?
2. **The return:** Have you found yourself revisiting that same place, situation or feeling, but from a different position? What had changed within you?
3. Your *winter* and *summer* phases (which we will visit more fully in Chapter 6): Looking back, do you think your first experience was during a *winter* phase (a time of doubt, introspection or challenge) and your return during a *summer* phase (a time of clarity, achievement or expansion)?
4. **Lessons and growth:** What did this full-circle moment reveal to you about your own personal growth cycle? How did it shape your understanding of progress and transformation?
5. **Future awareness:** How can recognising these cycles help you trust your journey and embrace future phases with more ease?

TAKE SOME TIME TO REFLECT, and if you feel called to, write down your own full-circle story — you may be surprised at how much clarity it brings.

. . .

Now, let's dive into why cycles — and the full-circle moments they bring — are so often misunderstood.

5
WHY ARE CYCLES MISUNDERSTOOD OR MISSING?

There is a missing narrative around cycles, precisely because women themselves have been 'missing' from history. This is no coincidence. It stands to reason that the erasure of women's voices has led to the erosion of cyclical wisdom — a direct correlation that has shaped the way we perceive growth, success, and even time itself.

In Pip Williams' historical fiction novel, *The Dictionary of Lost Words*, it's 1857 and the main character, Esme, sits beneath the table in the Scriptorium as the men around her compile the Oxford English Dictionary. Unseen and unheard, she begins to collect words that are misplaced, disregarded, or neglected — words that the men deem irrelevant or unimportant. The first word Esme rescues is "bondmaid", which she discovers means a female servant or a woman bound to service without wages. The absence of this word from the dictionary speaks volumes — not just about language, but about the erasure of women's experiences.

. . .

Fast forward to today, and this erasure still persists as Caroline Criado-Perez[1] highlights in *Invisible Women*, 75% of the world's unpaid work is carried out by women — a statistic that only worsened during the pandemic. So while the word "bondmaid" may have been missing from the Oxford Dictionary 200 years ago, the reality it describes remains very much present.

Although *The Dictionary of Lost Words* is a work of fiction, it is based on historical truth. Women were indeed involved in the compilation of the Oxford Dictionary, yet they remained on the periphery — unseen and unheard. When the dictionary was first published in 1884, a celebratory dinner was held. The men were invited to dine; the women were merely allowed to watch from the sidelines.

Why? Because men were considered superior, and so were masculine-based principles, values and even words. Women, by contrast, were deemed inferior — along with our feminine-based principles, values and language. This historical reality is a stark reminder that the exclusion of the feminine (and the cyclical) — from words to work to worth — is not an accident. It is a pattern, one that continues to shape our world today.

Meryl Streep recently stated, *"We've grown up learning the language of men, and now they must learn the language of women."* A crucial part of this language is the cyclical nature of life—a concept that was widely understood in ancient times, as seen in Latin and Greek, however, in today's world, the concept of the cycle is more commonly associated with economic growth cycles than with nature or the rhythms of our own lives. And why is that? Because men — not women — interpreted and defined the meaning of the modern world

---

1. *Invisible Women*, Exposing the Gender Data Gap by Caroline Criado-Perez

we live in. Women, along with feminine principles, values and nature itself, were deemed unimportant, inferior and something to be overpowered.

"Every time women *acquired any status, power, or asserted their divinity or spirituality in any way, it got crushed. It happens over and over again — they get slandered, dismissed, and horribly represented because they are women."*
Nikki Marmery

In researching her novel *Lilith*, author Nikki Marmery uncovered a familiar pattern. She realised that the biblical tale of Lilith — often cast as a night demon and Adam's first wife — wasn't just one woman's story, but a reflection of every woman's story. This insight led her to weave in the voices of other overlooked or maligned figures like Norea (Noah's wife), Jezebel and Mary Magdalene, crafting a bold fictional reimagining of the Bible. These women's stories had long been missing—or worse, grossly misrepresented.

From religious texts to historical books, women — and feminine principles — have consistently been missing, misunderstood or dismissed. This is a cycle in itself, repeating over and over again, erasing the great mother, the feminine and the cyclical from the mainstream narrative. *The Dictionary of Lost Words*[2] highlights 'the lost narrative hidden between the lines of a history written by men.'

That lost narrative is feminine and cyclical by nature. It also struck me that the main character, Esme, had lost her mother — a recurring theme in many historical fiction books. Esme's attempt to reconnect

---

2. *The Dictionary of Lost Words* by Pip Williams

with the feminine leads her to collect the lost words of women, scattered on the floor of the Scriptorium. And aren't we all doing this in some way?

As WOMEN, we intuitively know that the feminine — and the cycle — is missing. We feel the absence of the cyclical in a world that prioritises the linear, and we instinctively try to reconnect with it. The cycle is more than just a pattern — it is a mentor, a guide and even a mother to us throughout our lives. When we truly understand and embrace it, the cycle becomes something even more assuring, safe, and comforting than the linear line ever could be. In other words, the cycle holds us in a way that the linear line simply cannot.

BOTH RELIGION and agriculture are two of the primary reasons women lost control of their own stories. *If Women Rose Rooted*'[3] author Sharon Blackie explores how this shift occurred, particularly as religion — originating from the Middle East — made its way into Western culture. In her highly acclaimed book, which I recommend every woman to read, Blackie presents a compelling premise: the ownership of women coincided with the ownership of land. As societies moved from communal, land-based living to systems of ownership and control, women — who were once the guardians of the land and its wisdom — were gradually disempowered, silenced and erased from their own narratives.

"BEFORE THE CONCEPT *of land ownership, right back to the very conceptualisation of what the natural world is and what women are... because of this very act of giving birth and the more cyclical, rhythmical,*

---

3. *If Women Rose Rooted*, A Life Changing Journey of Authenticity and Belonging by Sharon Blackie

seasonal ways in which women's physical life expresses itself — we were separated from rationality and linear thinking."
Dr Sharon Blackie[4]

SHE REMINDS us the feminine force carries a slower, deeper, and more embodied wisdom — and it's when we begin to interrogate ancient stories, we can truly reconnect to ourselves as women. We can learn this wisdom from our Native American sisters, and I highly recommend *Braiding Sweetgrass*[5] by Robin Wall Kimmerer — a book gifted to me by one of my soul sisters and retreat co-host of several years, Gemma Williams.

BUT DR BLACKIE also reminds us that we can find traces of these ancient feminine stories much closer to home—within the Gaelic traditions of Ireland and Scotland, and even in the English and Welsh myths that have survived. By reconnecting with these stories, the land and our cyclical nature, we can begin to reclaim the wisdom that has always been ours.

"WE CAN LOOK beyond the surface of the hidden narrative, which is feminine, and the cyclical nature of women as the creative power of the universe."
Dr Sharon Blackie[6]

---

4. She Rebel Radio®, Episode 135 https://sites.libsyn.com/210074/if-women-rose-rooted-with-sharon-blackie
5. *Braiding Sweetgrass, Indigenous Wisdom, Scientific Knowledge and the Teaching of Plants* by Robin Wall Kimmerer
6. *If Women Rose Rooted*, A Life Changing Journey of Authenticity and Belonging by Sharon Blackie, She Rebel Radio®, Episode 135 https://sites.libsyn.com/210074/if-women-rose-rooted-with-sharon-blackie

In 1928, Virginia Woolf[7] wrote, with both ambition and ambiguity, in *A Room of One's Own*: "Women's values are different from men's, and theirs are seen as more important than ours." To illustrate her point, Woolf has been criticised for generalising, particularly when comparing men's love for football with women's love for fashion. But we must consider the historical context in which *A Room of One's Own* was written — and the limited resources available to Woolf, even as a privileged woman.

DESPITE HER SIGNIFICANT research on women and literature, Woolf encountered a frustrating truth: most writing *about* women had been written by men. Even with her literary genius and access to her father's extensive library — a collection greater than that of Cambridge University, where her brothers were educated — she too was in the dark about the true language of women.

WE HAD LOST control of our own stories centuries before, and with that loss, we became disconnected from our feminine-based principles and values. It is perhaps no coincidence that Woolf herself lost her mother at just 13 years old, a defining moment of grief that may have deepened her sense of disconnection from the feminine. Woolf's frustration was not just intellectual — it was deeply personal.

THE MISUNDERSTANDING, omission, and even demonisation of the feminine narrative has led to the misinterpretation of cycles, recurrence and the natural fluctuations of life. As a result, we have become deeply disconnected from ourselves, our distinct phases, and the cyclical nature of our existence. This disconnection affects us both individually and collectively — like a bird trying to fly with only one wing.

---

7. *A Room of One's Own* by Virginia Woolf

THE SYSTEMS and structures that continue to shape our world were created by men and entrenched in masculine-based principles. These systems remain rigidly linear, prioritising constant growth, control, and predictability — and they are not working for the collective whole. Without the balance of cyclical wisdom, we find ourselves pushing, striving, and burning out, rather than embracing the natural rhythms of expansion, contraction, rest, and renewal.

RECLAIMING the feminine and cyclical is not just about creating more balance and deeper insights within our own personal growth journeys — it is about reshaping the world into one that works in harmony with nature, humanity and our true selves.

REFLECTION:

- What has this chapter revealed to you about what has been missing in your life?
- How do you feel about embracing more of the cyclical wisdom that has been overlooked or dismissed?

NEXT, we step into this wisdom more fully as we meet The Genius Wheel® — a dual-layered framework that integrates both the seasonal cycle and the 7-year personal growth cycle. If it resonates with you, we can also weave in the rhythms of the moon cycle and/or your menstrual cycle (if still present). We begin by first understanding the 12-month seasonal cycle, also known as the *Wheel of the Year* — an ancient guide to the natural flow of life and transition.

6
THE SEASONAL CYCLE (12-MONTH CYCLE)

The seasonal cycle reflects the earth's full 360-degree rotation on its axis. Many of us are familiar with the commercial aspects of the seasons, but it's in nature that we truly see their impact. Modern Paganism follows the Wheel of the Year for seasonal worship, though there is no clear evidence that traditional pagans used this specific system. However, they did revere nature and worship multiple deities rather than a single masculine archetype. It naturally follows that this was a space where women (and nature) held more power and were more widely worshipped.

THE GENIUS WHEEL® is a dual-layered framework that integrates both the seasonal cycle and the 7-year personal growth cycle. If it resonates with you, you can also weave in the rhythms of the moon and/or your menstrual cycle (if present). For now, please just familiarise yourself with *Image A* below.

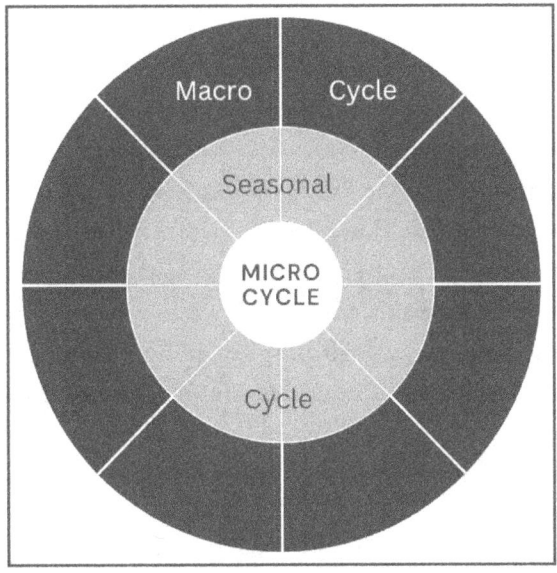

Image A

THERE ARE 3 circles within the image. The outer circle is what's called the macro cycle which is your 7-year personal growth cycle which you will learn more about in Chapter 7. The middle circle is the seasonal cycle which means the season we are in externally and this relates to this chapter. The smallest circle is the micro cycle which is either the moon phase or your menstrual cycle, you will learn more about this in Chapter 8. For now, we will focus on understanding more about the seasonal cycle (middle circle).

EVEN IN THE middle of a city, we respond to the changing seasons. We may notice the Christmas lights going up in December or the colourful flags appearing in May to mark festival season. Where I live in Brighton, around the *Summer Solstice* — the longest day of the year — street buskers grow louder, and young students celebrate exam results and the end of college, sometimes getting inebriated and performing handstands outside shop windows.

IN LOCKDOWN, like many I was unable to escape abroad and forced to stay here in the UK for the full turn of the year. Eventually, I chose to spend most of my time down in Cornwall with better beaches than Sussex. Prior to this and since I'd left legal practice as a criminal defence lawyer, I'd been tracking how the seasons impacted my energy. Back then, I was 'too busy' to notice the seasonal cycle — except for planning my annual leave and organising the Christmas out-of-hours rota.

BEFORE CORNWALL, I lived by the beach in Shoreham and as I began to slow down, I noticed the transitional nature of the beach at the turn of each season. On my daily walks, I listened closely to the embodied wisdom within myself. In the *winter*, my energy was lower and the sun rose in the east giving birth to later mornings and bright pink sunrises. I also noticed trucks would arrive on the beach to turn the stones. In *spring*, as my energy and clarity rose, so did the flora and fauna, bursting into growth and blooming in shades of pink, purple, and white, ready for early *summer*. I felt ready to book courses, coaches, and retreats — finally, I was ready for the year ahead. The days grew longer, and the sun set later in the western sky. By late *summer*, I began to tire of the season's relentless energy. *Autumn* slowly introduced itself, as the intense *summer* heat faded, leaving plants scorched and the grass losing its vibrant green. The refined browns, oranges and reds remained until *winter* arrived again and all became stripped bare. My energy dropped a little deeper, finding time to pause as the pebbles of the beach glittered with frost. That was until the whole cycle started again. It happens every year without fail.

. . .

"THE BEACH IS *a space of continuous transition. There is a lack of being static and that reminds us that change is constant."*
Lizzi Larbalestier[1]

THE *SPRING and autumn* are more transitional, they tend to bring balance and more softness than the fullness of *summer* and the emptiness of *winter*. In *spring*, the energy builds up and in *autumn*, it drops down. I work in the transitional space and being a Libra, transition, movement and balance are my favourite energies.

SPRING AND AUTUMN are also a great time to do the transitional work which is why I host retreats mostly at these times of year. Although the pause of January can also be a great time. When we slow down, we can begin to notice how seasons transition from one phase into the other, which is exactly what happens during our own personal growth cycles.

USING The Seasons To Re-Orientate Ourselves

IMAGINE YOURSELF SOMEWHERE NEW — somewhere you have never been before, perhaps it's a new city or a forest walk. Suddenly, you realise you are lost and can't find that restaurant or place of beauty you were heading to. What is the first thing you would do? Look at a map or find somewhere familiar that you recognise.

THE TRUTH IS we all find ourselves lost at moments of our lives,

---

1. Lizzi Larbalesteir, Blue Health Coaching® / https://goingcoastal.blue/
She Rebel Radio, Episode 122 https://sites.libsyn.com/210074/how-blue-space-can-unlock-purpose-and-possibility-with-lizzi-l-from-going-coastal-blue

careers and businesses. Sometimes, we might look to family members or gurus to help us re-find our direction. But we can also use the seasons to re-orientate ourselves. Our ancestors were massively tuned into the seasons as their lives depended on it.

TO RE-ORIENTATE ourselves is to ascertain our position. It is to stop and consider our direction. Sometimes it includes noticing how far we've come, plotting how far we've left to go and considering the obstacles that may be further ahead. It is allowing ourselves a moment to gather our bearings. When was the last time you did that?

YOU MIGHT OFTEN THINK about where you stand in your career or within your organisation, but when was the last time you considered your positioning in life — *where am I, really?* We touched on this in Part I, when you identified which personal growth cycle you're currently in — the 6th, 7th, 8th, 9th or beyond. If the seasons follow a predictable, cyclical rhythm, then why wouldn't we? The truth is, we're too busy to notice these ever so important yet subtle shifts.

IN THE *WINTER* OF 2014 — unbeknownst to me, the *winter* phase of my 7-year personal growth cycle — I made a pivotal decision while on a flight to New York: I would leave my job as a lawyer. In the buildup to this change, uncertainty loomed. I felt unsure of my position at the firm where I had spent over a decade and even more uncertain about what the future held if I left. I had countless questions but no clear sense of direction and I was unable to orientate myself.

HAVING NOW CHARTED my path with The Genius Wheel®, I know there was much alignment behind this decision. We were in the physical season of *Samhain* (1st November to 21st December) which is the first half of *winter* (shown in the middle circle). This is also where I was within my 7-year personal growth cycle. The moon cycle was waning crescent which also corresponds with the season of *Samhain* (inner circle). *Samhain* as you will learn below connects us with the energy of *uncertainty* and I had a triple whammy of it. In fact, for almost a year before that, I knew something needed to change. I just didn't know what that looked like or how I was going to do it. This was a monumental decision, and represented a metaphorical death of sorts, and some may even call it a *'winter of the soul'* — I'd ended a cycle and my identity was ready to shift.

BELOW I'VE SHARED with you, an image of what my Genius Wheel looked like which was (of course) unbeknown to me at the time.

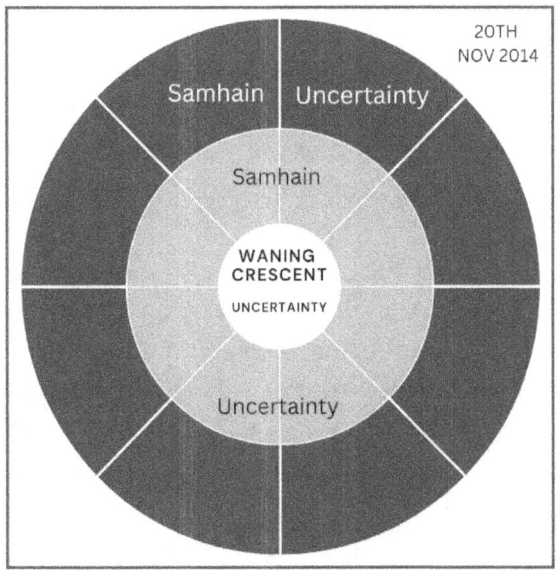

Image B

IN 2015, as *spring* came around — I was at the end of my 'gardening leave' from the law firm. I began to explore new ideas and businesses but still my energy was low as I was still in my macro cycle of *winter*. I'd burnt myself out and was unable, at the time, to pay attention to my 7-year growth cycle. But by the time the next *spring* came around (2016) — I had a much clearer sense of my direction and orientation. And that was because the *spring* part of my 7-year personal growth cycle was now in action. And then the *summer* came and so on.

SLOWLY, I became aware of the cyclical presence in my life and the impact it had on me. Like clockwork, I could trust an unfolding that would occur. This is something I began to share and raise awareness of for my coaching clients i.e. don't make too many decisions in *winter* — all will become much clearer in the spring, and so forth.

IN 2017, I intuitively stopped taking the contraceptive pill and thanks to the work of Red School[2], I then became aware of the cyclical presence of my menstrual cycle and the seasons showing up within that too. We will explore this further in Chapter 8.

AND EVENTUALLY, I began hosting an online empowerment circle for the *spring and Autumn Equinox* and the *winter and Summer Solstice*. You could say the seasons began to act as my own personal mentor and guide. We can be informed and guided by the seasons as we navigate the seasons of our life, our businesses and importantly our 7-year personal growth cycle. I began to really understand that our thoughts, feelings and identities are not created in isolation — they are deeply intertwined with the environment and natural forces around us. The elements don't just exist outside of us; they actively inform how we perceive and experience life.

---

2. https://www.redschool.net/

> "THERE IS no separation between subjectivity and the elements. The elemental forces inform and elevate subjectivity."
> **John O'Donoghue**[3]

FOR ME THE final piece of the jigsaw was understanding that there are actually 8 distinct seasons and not simply 4. Let's meet them...

---

[3]. *Anam Cara*, Spiritual Wisdom from the Celtic World John O'Donoghue

The 8 Phases:

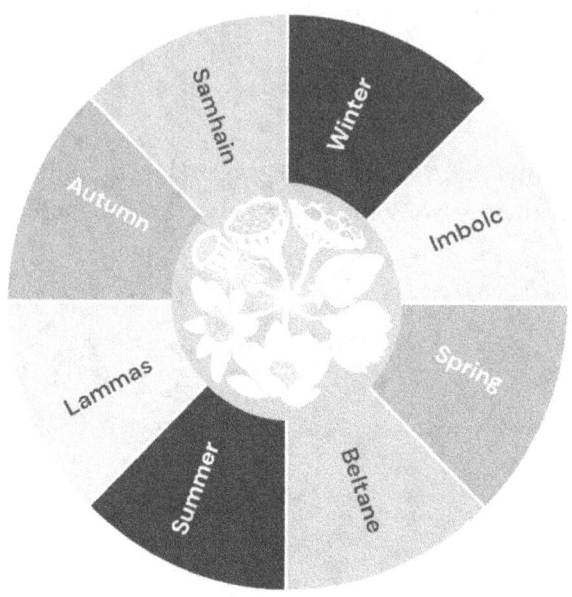

Image C

The Crossover Seasons:

SAMHAIN IS on the 1st November and means *summer*'s end or November in Irish. It marks the initiation of *winter* and our darkest months. *Imbolc* is on the 1st February and means the belly of the mother. It marks the initiation of *spring* and returning of the light. *Beltane* is on the 1st May and means 'fires of the bel'. It marks the initiation of *summer* and the power of heat from the sun. *Lammas* is on the 1st August and means 'full loaf' and marks the initiation of *autumn* and fullness of that harvest. We will call these the crossover seasons. This is because for each you are crossing over from one season to the next. I.e. from *autumn* into *winter*, *winter* into *spring*, *spring* into *summer* and *summer* into *autumn*.

The Main Seasons:

Winter Solstice or *Yule* (21st December) marks the shortest day of the year and the longest night. It occurs when either of the earth's poles tilts the furthest away from the sun. *Spring Equinox* or *Ostara* (21st March) marks balance with 12 hours of equal day (light) and night (dark). The earth's axis tilts neither towards or away from the sun. It marks a transitional moment as from here, the daylight hours speed up.

Summer Solstice or *Litha* (21st June) marks the longest day of the year and the shortest night. It occurs when either of the earth's poles tilts closest to the sun. Stonehenge in Wiltshire is believed to have been built as a giant calendar to mark the *Summer Solstice*. On this day, the sun rises in the northeast, aligning with the monument's Heel Stone. This remarkable feat by our Neolithic ancestors demonstrates their ability to orient themselves within the seasons and the cycle of the year.

Autumn Equinox or *Mabon* (21st September) marks abundance and like the *Spring Equinox*, a moment of balance with 12 hours of equal night and day. The earth's axis tilts neither towards or away from the sun. It marks another transitional moment, as the light starts to disappear resulting in shorter days until we again reach the *Winter Solstice*.

THE POLARITY PRINCIPLE (Chapter 4) also applies here as one phase cannot exist without its polar opposite:

Two opposing but complementary forces where one cannot exist without the other.

Samhain is the twin and polar opposite of *Beltane*.
Winter Solstice is the twin and polar opposite of the *Summer Solstice*.
Lammas is the twin and polar opposite of *Imbolc*.
Autumn Equinox is the twin and polar opposite of the *Spring Equinox*.

The Wheel of the Year:

These 8 phases and turning of the seasonal wheel is known as the Wheel of the Year and it's these 8 phases that we will use to mirror your own 7-year personal growth cycle. You may have noticed above, how each of the 8 phases is referenced in accordance with the light, i.e. how much light we are receiving, whether it is in balance, returning or disappearing. This occurs in an entirely predictable pattern which is why when we use the 8 phases as our guide for our own personal growth cycle, we can consider how full of light we may feel at any one time.

Yet, it is important to remember that the loss of light is not always a negative thing. There is great wisdom in the void, the darkness, and the unseen realms of black matter. We must challenge our belief system and question why we associate the absence of light with something 'lesser'. As we move along Part II of this book, you will begin to understand your own personal growth cycle but please be patient, as it takes time.

To gather a greater understanding of each of the 8 phases, I invite you to join my Substack[4] community.

The Energy Wheel:

It's important to remember which crossover season belongs to which main season and below I've given each of the 8 phases a particular energy.

---

4. luluminns.substack.com

SAMHAIN **BELONGS WITH** *WINTER*: Uncertainty and elimination. *Imbolc* **belongs with** *spring*: Space and curiosity. *Beltane* **belongs with** *summer*: Ignition and maximising. *Lammas* **belongs with** *autumn*: Fullness and refinement.

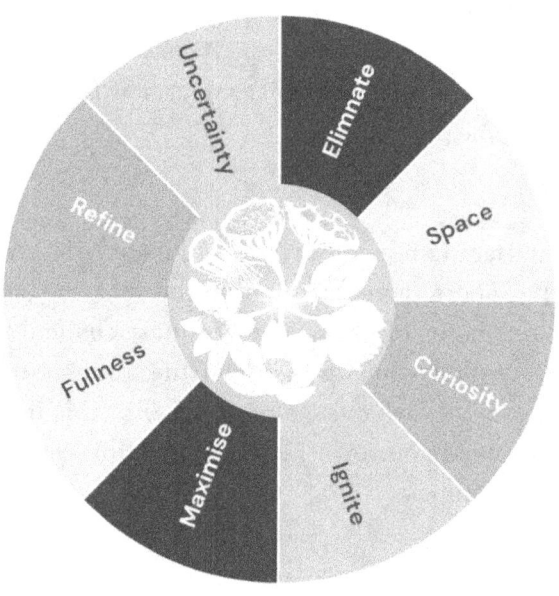

Image D

THIS IS because when you know what season you are in personally (your macro cycle), you'll understand what energy you can leverage which we will explore in further detail shortly. If we remember *the seasonal promise,* that *spring* always follows *winter,* we can also predict what energy comes next which is a powerful tool to orient ourselves within. The seasons run in the same order every single time, just like breathing, so let's take a moment to orient ourselves within that.

REFLECTION:
Exercise A — breathing practice
The practice below helps us tune into the 4 main seasons and how they flow from one to the other.

Spring is breathing in. Holding at the top of your breath is *summer*. Breathing out is *autumn*. Pausing at the bottom is *winter*.

1. Breathe in for 4 seconds. Hold at the top. Breath out for 4 seconds. Pause at the bottom.
2. Do this 3 to 4 times.
3. Place a hand on your belly.
4. Repeat again 3 or 4 times, bringing the seasons to your mind's eye.
5. Breathe in for 4 seconds - feel the rising of *spring*.
6. Hold at the top - feel the expansion of *summer*.
7. Breathe out for 4 seconds - feel the drop in (contraction) and release of *autumn*.
8. Pause at the bottom - feel the stillness and emptiness of *winter*.

EXERCISE B — SEASONAL REFLECTION:
Reflect on how the seasons shift where you live? What do you notice, what changes and when? How does it make you feel?

Next, we will dive into each of the seasons more intentionally.

Winter (stopping or pausing): uncertainty and elimination

> **"I want to curl up in a ball and bury my body into the earth, But she whispered, "it's not your time".**

> I want to hide deep in the forest so no one can find me.
> But she whispered, "it's not your time".
>
> — It's not your time by Gemma Williams[5]

The phase of *winter* is in 2 parts: *Samhain* (*uncertainty*) and *Winter Solstice* (*elimination*).

I'VE CHOSEN to start the cycle here because *winter* and the darkness is where everything starts. Death, birth and rebirth are all one of the same. If we think of our own birth - each of us starts within the darkest and often the safest of spaces - inside the wombs of our mothers. It is here our rooting to the external world really begins. And it's within the *winter phase* of our personal growth cycles that we gain greater wisdom, maturity and growth which we can use to root and re-root ourselves in. That is if we allow ourselves to.

FINDING the *winter* moments of our lives is often the most easy to identify, because they have a *'before and after'* moment. When we consciously do our rooting and re-rooting in *winter* and are brave enough to pause what needs pausing, the *seasonal promise* is that our *spring* shall be twice as bright.

THE PHASE of *winter* begins with a *Samhain* (1st November) and a period of *uncertainty*. *Samhain* is also the name for November in Irish, marking the end of *summer* and the harvest season and the start of the darker half of the year. Starting on the 31st October (also Halloween), the pagan fire festival of *Samhain* would sometimes last for up to 3 days. It was believed that at this time of the year, the veil between our world and the spirit world was permeable, a time when

---

5. Gemma Williams, Yoga Teacher Training / https://gemyoga.co.uk/

our ancestors could more easily reach us. We can also interpret this as a time when our connection to our deepest intuition and true essence — who we are meant to be — is at its strongest.

For the purposes of The Genius Wheel®, I'm going to share with you how each of the 8 seasons relates to a chakra (energy wheel in the body), the moon cycle, cardinal or intercardinal directions, and the time. You'll also discover the element and energy associated with each phase, helping you to embody all eight stages more fully.

Samhain represents our soul star chakra, which is connected to the spirit world and 'all that is'. A chakra is an energy wheel (connected to yoga philosophy) most often within the body, but the soul star chakra is approximately 6 inches above our head. *Samhain* represents the waning crescent moon just before it goes dark (new moon). The direction is north west. The time is 9pm. This is a crossover phase where the element of water (*autumn*) meets the element earth (*winter*). When '*water* meets *earth*' it creates a sludginess, or slipperiness and a feeling of unease, *uncertainty* or even excitement as we step into the *unknown*. This phase represents our divine connection and guidance supporting us to re-adjust our journeys to more purpose, alignment and fulfilment. This is a place our willing or rational mind is not always willing to go.

In Buddhism and other spiritual traditions, the lotus flower is a symbol of awakening and it blooms in the muckiest and muddiest of swamps. Its roots begin under the swamp water and when the buds reach their way to the surface they burst forth with pink or white flowers. We can think of *Samhain* as this part of our personal growth cycle. It may feel like the muckiest and muddiest of swamps but it's full of life, the benefits of which we may be unable to see.

. . .

When we are uncertain, we can feel 'unsafe and unrooted' and experience a lack of clarity, anxiety and frustration of what is to come next. It can feel like waiting at an invisible train station or airport, not knowing the destination we are destined for. Our intuition or soul is trying to reach us.

This phase also relates to the premenstrual phase of our menstrual cycles. We can feel a rising sense of anxiety and waiting with uncertainty. The authors of *Wild Power*[6] describe the premenstrual phase as 'being on the cliff edge' and 'clawing our way' until we can finally see over the edge.

---

6. *Wild Power, Discover the Magic of your Menstrual Cycle* by Alexandra Pope and Sjanie Hugo Wurlitzer

CASE STUDY: *Jo Myles*

LOOKING AT OUR CASE STUDY, Jo had a number of significant shifts during her *Samhain* and *winter* phases. Firstly, within her 4th personal growth cycle, (aged 21 to 28), in 2003 to 2004 Jo was working as a fashion buyer for Laura Ashley. During her *Samhain* and *winter* phase, she decided to leave this job and found a similar role at Warehouse. This phase brought a growing dissatisfaction with the fast fashion industry, particularly its lack of sustainability and poor working conditions. Jo's disillusionment planted a seed of change — she realised she wanted to disrupt the industry and forge her own path which she did during her *spring* phase.

FAST FORWARD 14 years to 2017–2018: Jo, now a mother of 3 and running a successful business, was suddenly faced with a life-altering cancer diagnosis. The news prompted a deep period of reflection — on her life, her health, and the balance between motherhood, work, and self. This period coincided with the *winter* phase of her 6th personal growth cycle (ages 35 to 42), a time often marked by uncertainty and elimination. What began as a brief course of treatment soon evolved into something far more intense and gruelling. By July 2018, Jo made the difficult decision to close her business, *3 Blonde Bears*, aptly named after her children. The closure marked the end of a significant chapter, but — as she had done before — Jo used this ending to re-root herself in deeper truth, emerging from loss with renewed clarity and purpose.

WHAT ALWAYS FOLLOWS *Samhain* and the energy of *uncertainty*, is the *Winter Solstice* phase and energy of *elimination*. There is a 'before and after' of our *winter* phase and it's usually characterised by a literal or metaphorical death and/or a loss which results in a shift of identity. This can include the loss or departure from a significant job or vocation, the closure or liquidation of a business, the breakdown of an important relationship, or the loss of a loved one — or even a significant part of them. It may also involve a serious health diagnosis or condition, the transition of menopause, and more. At times, several of these challenges may arise at once. Sometimes everything and nothing is wrong all at the same time.

WINTER SOLSTICE MARKS the darkest day of the year and the gradual returning of the light. The root chakra represents this phase, located at the base of the spine, it represents safety and security, much like the roots of a tree anchoring us to the earth. The moon is dark (the new moon). The time is midnight. The direction is north and the element is earth. It is the menstruation and bleeding phase of our menstrual cycle. There can be a feeling of being held by mother earth. What once felt unclear now begins to reveal itself, showing us what can no longer remain as we move into the next phase — whether we choose it or not.

WE DON'T REALLY TALK about death in the UK but it is something that brings us closer to the truth of ourselves. Losing something or someone who held aspects of our identity means we are left with the gift of rooting ourselves deeper into who we really are.

THE *WINTER* PHASE can feel bleak and we may experience pain, loss, grief and turbulence but being able to find our centre within that is key. We can pause where possible and re-root ourselves within the shift that has occurred. Often we can begin to stand freer from default behaviours and to tune into a deeper truth of belonging to ourselves. If we allow it, we can begin to free ourselves from the restraints that disconnect us from our true selves and our innate genius. We develop less tolerance for inauthenticity, become more unapologetically ourselves, and reveal the truth to others with greater ease and confidence. As we shed self-imposed limitations, we also become less bound by the expectations of others.

WE CAN SPEND a significant amount of time resisting the *winter* phase of our lives instead of simply being brave enough to step into it. *Winter* represents the void. An empty space and sometimes feeling empty goes right along with it. Everything and nothing feels wrong. If we bring acceptance and/or conscious awareness to the void and willingly step into it, we can bring in more peace and more acceptance. We can give ourselves permission to pause and what follows is a more energised *spring*. As the truth is, no matter what we do — *spring* always follows *winter*. Yet if we resist, fight and overthink *winter* — we can end up exhausted and burnt out by the time *spring* comes around.

IF THE ABOVE WORDS RESONATE, you may be in your *winter* phase right now. Our *winter* phase lasts for 21 months and consists of both *Samhain*: uncertainty and *winter*: elimination. You will find out more about your macro cycle, the part of your 7-year personal growth cycle in Chapter 7. Let us first turn to how to harness the power of this phase.

How to Harness the Power of your *Samhain* and *Winter* Phase:

Winter is generally not the time for new projects or taking on big risks. It is a time to rest, pause and nurture stability. How can we get more comfortable with uncertainty and/or consciously eliminate the things that are shaping our identity but no longer feel like a good fit?

This is a powerful time for turning inward — to reflect, to write, perhaps even to begin that book you've been meaning to start. Embrace the quieter rhythm of the season: hibernate a little, cook nourishing meals at home, and allow stillness to become a practice in itself. Gentle movement practices like Qi Gong, Yin Yoga, hot yoga, and breathwork can support this inward journey, especially when paired with grounding postures such as spinal twists and other elimination poses.

During this time, focus your yoga and meditation on connecting with both your soul star and root chakras — bridging the spiritual with the physical. Strengthening your root chakra is especially important now, helping you to cultivate a sense of safety, security, and deep presence within your body. There are many supportive resources available online, including YouTube videos tailored for root chakra work — I'll also be sharing a special *Samhain* and *winter* meditation within the Substack[7] group to guide you further.

Journal about any uncertainty you are feeling. What are you in control of? What are you not in control of? What are you feeling certain and uncertain about? What parts of your identity would you

---

[7] luluminns.substack.com

like to 'stand free' from? What obligations or aspects of self no longer feel a good fit? What can you consciously eliminate?

DURING MY LAST *Samhain* and *winter* phase, I went through a profound clearing of my home of 11 years and even sold all my furniture. Extreme, I know, but it was deeply transformative. This season invites that kind of radical release; it's an ideal time to work with a coach or shamanic teacher to rewire your roots, shift long-held trauma, or dismantle limiting beliefs. If that resonates, feel free to reach out — I'm here if you'd like support. You might also consider working with a personal organiser to help you physically clear space, which often mirrors the internal work. For inspiration, I highly recommend the documentary *The Minimalists* — it beautifully explores the power of letting go.

CONSIDER, what truths are revealing themselves to you now? And get ready for the next phase: *Imbolc* (space) and *spring* (curiosity).

SPRING (WALKING OR MOVING): **Space and Curiosity**

"*Eastern sun melt the cold from my bones, curtain rise, take the darkness from my eyes, breathing in, pulling life into my lungs, As a child, I am born again.*"
Eastern Sun, Song by Ayla Nereo

The phase of *spring* is in 2 parts: *Imbolc (space)* and the *Spring Equinox (curiosity)*. We begin with *Imbolc* (belly of the mother) and the new *space* which emerges after the *winter*. *Imbolc* dates back to the 10th century and recognises the first stirrings of *spring* due to coinciding with the lambing season. Many of the ewes would start lactating at this time, providing fresh milk — a vital source of nourishment after the harsh *winter* months. It's on 1st February and marks the mid-way point between the *Winter Solstice* and *Spring Equinox*.

Imbolc represents fertility, new life and stepping into a new space but things can feel difficult and we can feel vulnerable. The saying 'nature abhors a vacuum' means that unfilled spaces go against the law of both physics and nature. Every space will eventually need to be filled with something. *Imbolc* is often when we feel or need the space but don't yet know what will come to fill it. There is a hint of *spring* in the air but we don't feel quite there yet and how it manifests will be different for each and every one of us.

For the purposes of The Genius Wheel®, *Imbolc* represents the sacral chakra (orange) which is below the belly button and connects us with sensuality and creativity. *Imbolc* represents the waxing crescent moon just *after* the dark or the new moon. The direction is north east. The time is 3am, also known as the 'witching hour'. This is a crossover phase where the element of earth (*winter*) begins to meet the element of air (*spring*). It is the element of air meeting earth, from our roots which stirs up and energises new beginnings. It is the moment before the dawn of a new day. We can start to bring in fertile new ideas and new manifestations. Whilst this phase represents a new season of hope and growth it is one we haven't actually created yet — we may feel different but our day to day experience hasn't necessarily caught up with us.

IN IRELAND, 1st February marks St Brigid's Day, now recognised with an official bank holiday. Brigid, before she became a saint, was revered as an ancient Irish goddess of spring — the youthful maiden who emerges to take the place of the *winter* crone, known as the Cailleach. Her day symbolises renewal, rebirth, and the gradual return of light.

AROUND THIS SAME TIME, the Chinese New Year is celebrated, falling on the first new moon between 20th January and 21st February. This major festival also marks a shift in energy and season. It begins with the Lantern Festival, a celebration of light and the start of a new lunar cycle. Each year in the Chinese zodiac is represented by an animal and an element, offering a unique symbolic character to the months ahead.

IN AMERICA, 2nd of February represents groundhog day signifying when the groundhog exits its burrow to see if *spring* has arrived but often it will need to burrow back into hibernation. This is a good metaphor for us and if we are also ready to step into the new beginnings, new ideas and new manifestations that *spring* has to offer or if we need to stay a little longer in the undoing of old patterns and manifestations from the past?

THIS PHASE ALSO REPRESENTS, a day or two after our menstrual bleed where we feel a new energy but still a little tired so we need to tread carefully. Our very first *Imbolc* is coming out of the womb, into the physical world — we need lots of nurturing and caring from our mothers and caregivers so nurturing ourselves as well as our new ideas is key during this phase.

CASE STUDY CONTINUED: *Jo Myles*

FOLLOWING her cancer diagnosis and treatment, Jo was already on a path of transformation, rediscovering her creative roots and embracing a new role as a full-time maker and artist. As she prepared to enter the *Imbolc* phase of her 7th personal growth cycle (genius phase), she felt ready to step more fully into this new chapter of her life. However, during this time of renewal, her relationship with her husband and father of her children, began to unravel. Despite the emotional challenges, reconnecting with her creativity became a source of strength for Jo. It allowed her to re-root herself in a deeper truth, aligning her life more authentically with her artistic passion and personal values.

IF WE COMPARE this to Jo's *Imbolc/spring* phase of her 5th personal growth cycle, Jo was not only managing a team of over 35 people for her business but she also won multiple awards. Whilst the business in itself wasn't new — it was in a new phase.

IN 2000, at the age of 22, Jo Myles had already completed her degree in textiles and was on the brink of entering her 4th personal growth cycle. As a student, she secured an internship with the renowned fashion designer, Alexander McQueen, marking the early stages of her career.

JO'S ROLE at McQueen expanded rapidly, and before long, she was at the centre of the brand's prestigious catwalk shows — turning initial sketches into finished garments, overseeing fittings, managing the archive, and even leading a team of interns, all while still remarkably young. Her natural leadership and creative instinct stood out from the start, and this professional rise mirrored a powerful inner shift.

When she began at McQueen, she was in the spring phase of her 4th cycle (June 1998 to April 1999) — a time of renewal and fresh starts. This energetic surge carried her into the Beltane phase, where her passion for fashion, creativity, and management was truly ignited.

THE PHASE of *spring* always follows *Imbolc* and the feeling of *space* and new beginnings. The energy of *spring* is one of a rising *curiosity*. We are keen to explore further, learn and seek out new opportunities. This is where we begin to physically manifest the energy of rebirth.

THE *SPRING EQUINOX* marks balance of day and night and is the transition point that creates longer days and shorter nights. The solar plexus chakra (yellow) represents this phase, located above the belly button and below the chest, it represents our power centre. The moon is in the first quarter. The time is 6am. The direction is east (where the sun rises) and the element is air which stirs up new energy. It is the follicular and building up phase of our menstrual cycle. We feel energised and *curious*.

SPRING IS the time to say YES and set clear intentions. We have more colour and more vision yet can still lack maturity. Remember the goddess Brigid of Ireland, *spring* still represents this archetype and the young maiden. We can say yes to too many things, find that we lack focus and later become overwhelmed by the commitments we've made during this time. We may also be selfish, excited about our new projects, talking about them incessantly and not realising others are not quite as enthusiastic. It's a great time to meet new people and create new relationships. We are more sociable and more fun but still learning how and need to be open to making mistakes. Now we can pick up the pace and finally move forward with much greater ease - trusting that our focus of interest will become clearer over time. Phew, thank god for that!

. . .

IF THE ABOVE WORDS RESONATE, you may be in your *spring* phase right now. Our *spring* phase lasts for 21 months and consists of both *Imbolc* (*space*) and *spring* (*curiosity*). You will find out more about your macro cycle, this part of your 7-year personal growth cycle in Chapter 7. Let us first turn to how to harness the power of this phase.

HOW TO HARNESS the power of *Imbolc* and our *spring* phase:

SPRING IS a great time for new projects and taking on risks. It's a time for movement, play and bold new interests. We must remember to allow the energy to build and not run before we can walk. We are still learning how and as such can be open to being taken advantage of by others.

THIS MIGHT BE a time when you are nurturing new ideas or have started a new business which can be fragile so take care to only share with those who will support you fully and perhaps be wary of those who may take advantage of the things that you don't yet know.

START to get clear about your overall intentions or set clear goals. This is also a great time to move house, start a new course, business or side hustle. Write a blog or start that book you've been meaning to write (I wrote this book during the season of *winter* but my macro cycle of spring). Join a new community group or start dating again. Breathe in fresh air on nature walks and perhaps even set some intentions before you go. Create a new space in your office or at home. Balance poses in yoga are great, think eagle or standing bow. Try or recommit to balanced breathing exercises such as pranayama or fire breath anything that fires up your solar plexus.

. . .

JOURNAL about the space you need and what you are feeling curious about. What is emerging within you? What are you feeling energised and optimistic about? What would you like to learn more about? How can you embrace some new mistakes and lessons? What might you need to be more selfish about? And get ready for the next phase: *Beltane* (ignite) and *summer* (maximise).

SUMMER (SPEEDING UP OR RUNNING): **Ignite and Maximise**

I AM expanding. I AM maximising. I AM confident with my purpose and potential. WHEN THE WHEEL TURNS, I expand and I grow. I AM here to serve in only the way I can.
I am here to fully express my sacred gifts.

THE PHASE of *summer* is in 2 parts: *Beltane (ignite)* and *summer (maximise)*. We begin with *Beltane ('fires of Bel')*, and a period of *ignition*. The *Beltane* season (1st May) marks the very beginning of *summer*. An ancient Celtic word and festival, Bel is likely to be in reference to the Celtic sun god, Belenus. The *Beltane* festival is often commemorated with bonfires, maypole dancing, and performing fertility rituals. *Beltane* is the twin of *Samhain*, instead of *uncertainty* — we have certainty in what we wish to *ignite*.

FOR THE PURPOSES of The Genius Wheel®, *Beltane* represents the heart chakra (pink or green) and represents what lights our heart up. *Beltane* represents the waxing gibbous moon just before the full moon appears. The direction is south east. The time is 9am. This is a crossover phase where the element of air begins to meet the element of fire. When air is added to fire — the burn rate increases quickly — it ignites energy. Within our menstrual cycle, this is a few days before our ovulation phase. Expect to have more focus and a strong sense of passion and even beauty during *Beltane*.

BELTANE IS ALSO LINKED to the Roman goddess Flora, a nature goddess, overseeing the flowering abundance of the plants, gardens and new growth. Flora and *Beltane* are also linked to the May Queen and Brigid, the maiden who we've already met above. It's also a time of handfasting, a Pagan temporary or permanent marriage, highlighting that both commitment and abundance are key during this phase.

DURING *BELTANE*, enthusiasm, excitement and inspiration ensue as well as intense moments of enjoyment. Things really start to quicken and become stirred up. It is a time for nailing our colours to the mast and committing to the path we choose to *ignite*. Beltane is where we must stop dilly dallying around and be bold and intrepid in our commitment to something! Staying in indecision is not a good place for us to be - you must be intentional about the *little fires* you are creating and what it is you want to be known for.

CASE STUDY CONTINUED: *Jo Myles*

IN 2007, at just 28 years old and entering the *Beltane* phase of her 5th growth cycle, Jo took a bold step and started her own business from her kitchen table. Armed with only £5,000 in savings (about £9,000 today), she began crafting unique, personal gifts whilst balancing the demands of starting a family. Her creative spark and determination paid off — within just 16 months, she became one of the top-grossing partners on *Not On The High Street*.

BETWEEN 2012 AND 2014, *3 Blonde Bears* expanded into a team of 35 employees. Jo, now 35 and in the midst of her 6th personal growth cycle, relished her role as the creative leader of her team whilst also cherishing moments with her family. With a customer base of over 17,000, Jo had an intuitive connection to both the needs of mothers and children. Her company earned multiple awards, including *Not On The High Street*'s prestigious 2012 *Partner of the Year* award. *3 Blonde Bears*' projected turnover increased by 50%, and was also recognised as one of the most creatively disruptive companies in the *Startups 100* list for 3 consecutive years (2012–2014). These achievements occurred during Jo's *spring* into *Beltane* and *summer* phases, a period of approximately 32 months (10.5 months in each phase) — marked by creativity, innovation, and the flourishing of her business.

By 2021, at 42 years old, Jo was thriving in her 7th personal growth cycle, fully immersed in the vibrant *summer* phase of her journey. She had established herself as a successful independent international artist and maker, with her work featured on *Sky Arts* that year, and shortlisted for the prestigious *Glyndebourne Tour Art Competition*. In November of 2021, Jo co-founded *The Sussex Contemporary Ltd*[8], a platform designed to uplift and support Sussex-linked artists. As the creative director, her mission was clear: to share the knowledge, passion, and lessons she had garnered over two decades in the creative industries, whilst creating a supportive community for fellow Sussex artists.

The phase of *summer* always follows *Beltane* and the energy of *ignition*. The energy of the *summer* is about *maximising*, expanding and growing that with which we have already ignited in the previous phase of *Beltane*. *Summer* is the twin of *winter*, the deeper we've allowed rest and clearing out in *winter*, the more expansive our *summer* phase ought to be. Instead of *elimination*, we have *maximisation*.

Summer Solstice is the longest day of the year and the energy of the sun is at its peak. For the purposes of The Genius Wheel®, the throat chakra (blue) represents the *summer* phase and is a time when we are in full expression of ourselves. The moon is full. The direction is

---

8. https://www.thesussexcontemporary.co.uk/

south where we get the most sun and heat. The time is midday. The element is fire and it is the ovulation time of our menstrual cycle. This is a time, we are able to leave others with the impact of our authentic selves and to be unapologetic in what it is we stand for.

SUMMER IS the time for clear focus and to *maximise* our potential and purpose. It is a time for maturity, we have already learnt how and we can take ownership of our knowledge, power and ability. *Summer* itself is full of colour and vibrancy and we can create sustenance to bigger ideas, goals and plans. There is a richness, texture and depth to our work and our relationships. Commit to making it bigger and as great as possible. It's time to go big, or go home — maximise our input, value and double down on returns.

IF THE ABOVE WORDS RESONATE, you may be in your *summer* phase right now. Our *summer* phase tends to last approximately 21 months and consists of both *Beltane* (*ignite*) and *Summer Solstice* (*maximise*). You will find out more about your macro cycle, the part of your 7-year personal growth cycle in Chapter 7. Let us first turn to how to harness the power of this phase.

HOW TO HARNESS the power of *Beltane* and our *summer* phase:

SUMMER IS the time to commit and take on bigger risks. It's time for speeding up, taking action and following a more linear plan. We can use the power of our heart and throat connection to speak with power, market our ideas and galvanise others to follow our lead.

THIS MIGHT BE a time when you are confident in sharing something new with others, perhaps get help from someone to help you get clear about your marketing and message and what it is you are boldly sharing.

It's time to think big goals and a clear strategy on how you are going to get there. This is not a time for starting something new but more about bringing in wisdom, growth and fullness to that which you already know or have been practising in the previous phase. Build a team, hire a sales or marketing coach, get help with your messaging. Increase your network and impact in your field. Share your voice by speaking on stage, launching a webinar or start a newsletter on Substack or LinkedIn.

This phase is a great time for exercises that build strength and power! In Yoga — planks, warrior and the goddess pose are all great. You might want to consider Reformer pilates, HIIT workouts or even weight lifting. But don't forget the heart openers (camel pose and wild thing in yoga), and chanting and kirtan are also great for your throat chakra.

Journal about the clarity you have for your dreams, desires and things that spark your joy. What impact do you want to manifest and bring into being? Where is your passion and focus? What knowledge, power and ability can you openly share? What opinions and expertise can you leverage? What fires do you wish to ignite and commit too? What is the plan or strategy?

As *summer* is about commitment and action, you might also wish to complete this statement of intent:

I am focused on :

I AM COMMITTED TO :

MY ACTION IS :

THEN GET ready for the next phase: *Lammas* (fullness) and *autumn* (refinement).

AUTUMN (SLOWING DOWN): **fullness and refinement**

"SEASON OF MISTS *and mellow fruitfulness, Close bosom-friend of the maturing sun*"
   To Autumn by John Keats

THE PHASE of *autumn* is in 2 parts: *Lammas (fullness)* and *autumn (refinement)*. We begin with *Lammas*, and a period of *fullness*. The *Lammas* season (1st August) marks an initiation into *autumn* and represents the harvest of grains, fruit and vegetables which are now ripe and ready to eat. John Keats use of the word 'mellow' indicates ripeness, juiciness and sweetness. The word *Lammas* comes from an ancient English phrase meaning 'loaf mass'. Traditionally, in August a late *summer* festival with breads and cakes would take place to celebrate the harvest. *Lammas* is the twin of *Imbolc*, instead of *space* — we have *fullness*.

FOR THE PURPOSES of The Genius Wheel®, *Lammas* represents the third eye chakra which is the space in between and slightly above our eyebrows. It represents wisdom, insight and inner vision beyond ordinary sight. This phase is the waning gibbous moon which is immediately after the full moon. The direction is south-west. The time is 3pm — a time when we often feel full from lunch and long for a restful snooze in the warm, late *summer* sun. This is a crossover phase where the element of fire meets the element of water. It is the post ovulation part of our menstrual cycle.

DURING THIS PHASE, we start to slowly dampen down and extinguish the fires of our passion. The peak of *summer* — and ovulation — has passed. John Keats speaks of 'the soft dying day'. The vibrant hues of grass and *summer* flowers have faded, leaving imprints in the sun-scorched earth from fairgrounds, festivals and circus tents. But we can lean into the fullness — satisfied with our progress, content with reaping the rewards of our work, and embracing a sense of abundance and wholeness

THE IRISH GODDESS Áine is connected to *Lammas* and her presence lingers in *autumn* as the harvest goddess, ensuring the earth's abundance before *winter*'s arrival. She embodies the transition from *summer* warmth to *autumn's* golden fields.

AT *LAMMAS* we can slow down, celebrating the fullness of what we have achieved and begin to lean into some of the lessons from the challenges and opportunities experienced during the previous phase.

CASE STUDY CONTINUED: *Jo Myles*

In 2022, Jo was in the *Lammas* phase of her growth cycle and life was very full. Jo was able to celebrate the richness of her achievements. Her artwork was exhibited in *The Turner Contemporary Open*, and she was elected as director trustee of the *Ditchling Museum of Art + Craft* — both affirmations of her growing influence in the art world. Personally, her life had expanded too, as she found love again and embraced her new role as a mother of 5. However during her *autumn* phase, the relationship began to wane and she knew she needed to refine some of the situations she was experiencing. Prioritising everyone's needs above her own, she was unable to tend to this until her *winter* phase began and she was forced to.

The phase of the *autumn* always follows *Lammas* and the energy of *fullness*. The *autumn* phase is defined by *refinement*. The Autumn Equinox represents balance and the transition into longer nights and shorter days. The energy starts to wane. *Autumn* is the twin of *spring* and instead of the energy of *curiosity* and opening up to new opportunities, we have the energy of *refinement* where we close things off and create more boundaries for ourselves.

For the purpose of The Genius Wheel®, *autumn i*s represented by the crown chakra which is characterised by a bright white light at the top of our heads. The crown chakra is connected to divine wisdom, universal consciousness and greater self awareness and knowledge. The moon is in its 2nd (or last) quarter. The direction is west which is where the sun begins to set. The time is 6pm. This is the beginning of our premenstrual phase and a turning inwards of our energy. We step into the element of water (a metaphor for emotion) and may want to fully immerse ourselves here.

. . .

WATER EMBODIES FLOW, deep wisdom and intuition - just as water carves through rock over time, lived experience shapes our purpose and legacy as does our *autumn* phase. Water chooses the path of least resistance and here we can begin to distill the lessons of the past cycle - asking what we've learnt and how we need to refine into closer alignment with our purpose, our contribution and our identity. We are in transition - as all of our experiences, wisdom, and talents begin to converge. It is the culmination of our genius. Spiritual and emotional fulfillment again takes priority, along with a deeper connection to ourselves, and even more meaning.

THE WORD *AUTUMN* comes from the old English word 'hærfest' and is aptly the season for gathering the food of the land. *Autumn* is when we can harvest our genius and gather the fruits of our labour. In Greek mythology, Demeter is the goddess of grain, harvest and agriculture and her grief ties in with the dying of the crops and kidnap of her daughter Persephone into the underworld.

BEFORE WE DESCEND into the underworld and darker half of the year, we must refine and preserve our energy, trimming things down to what is and is not important. There is a level of maturity, responsible discernment and objective judgement required as we break away from the outward focus. We begin to ask and question all that we have learnt. We undo and unravel, setting boundaries and saying no to what no longer feels good for us. We must preserve a little of the harvest for ourselves. We are becoming self full and are essentially no longer needing to please others.

IF THE ABOVE WORDS RESONATE, you may be in your *autumn* phase right now. Our *autumn* phase tends to last approximately 21 months and consists of both *Lammas: fullness* and *autumn: refinement*. You will find out more about your macro cycle, and the relevant part of your 7-year personal growth cycle in Chapter 7. Let us first turn to how to harness the power of this phase.

HOW TO HARNESS the power of *Lammas* and our *autumn* phase:

AUTUMN IS about reaping the rewards from our earlier phase and a gradual turning inward. It's a time for slowing down, maturity and trimming away that which no longer feels good. We can use the wisdom from our upper chakras and deeper connection to connect with a greater universal plan and our genius phase.

THINK OF SAYING NO, creating boundaries, diving deeper into our emotions and intuition. One of my favourite activities is 'saying no to the NPTs' — these are the non-profitable, non-promotional and non-pleasurable tasks!

WE CAN ALSO APPLY MORE practical strategies such as the pareto principle, also known as the 80/20 rule in that 80% of benefits come from just 20% of the work. What is the 20% of what we are doing that is actually working? How can you double down on the 20% and get rid of the other 80% of work? It's a great time to gather interviews, testimonials and data from your clients or your team so you can distill the lessons.

REMEMBER in *Lammas* and *autumn* phase we should now be responsible by default due to the wisdom the cycle/s have bestowed upon us. We begin to preserve the lessons and distill our wisdom not erratically but gradually reducing and ensuring we keep the most important parts. It's important to be super intentional about it as *autumn* is a time we have more control than our *winter* phase of elimination.

. . .

This phase is a great time for water immersion, spa days, cold water or wild swimming. Or taking a trip to a waterfall. Take your journal, reflect and distill the lessons. Deep meditative practices or yoga nidra are also great. The work of Joe Dispenza[9] and his book breaking the habit of being yourself, connects our third eye to our pineal gland which is a gateway to higher consciousness. Breath work, visualisation and practising gratitude for the harvest season is essential. We can enhance our intuition and inner vision by doing all of the above.

Journal where you are feeling full and content. How can you apply the 80/20 rule? What questions can you sit with? What have you learnt about yourself? What boundaries can you say no to?

Refer to **Appendix B** (after the Acknowledgments section at the end of the book), for a full summary of the phases and corresponding energies, elements, moon cycles and more.

So now, you have been introduced to each of the 8 phases — let's see how these relate and show up within your 7-year personal growth cycle. This is the whole purpose of The Genius Wheel® and how it is you can connect and embody it — using it as your guide.

---

9. *Breaking the Habit of Being Yourself*, How to Lose your Mind and Create a New One by Joe Dispenza

7
YOUR MACRO CYCLE (THE 7-YEAR PERSONAL GROWTH CYCLE)

"7 is a fortuitous number to many people and religions."
LAURA SHEPHERD-ROBINSON —
The Square of Sevens

Your macro cycle is the largest circle on the outer side of your Genius Wheel and represents your 7-year personal growth cycle.

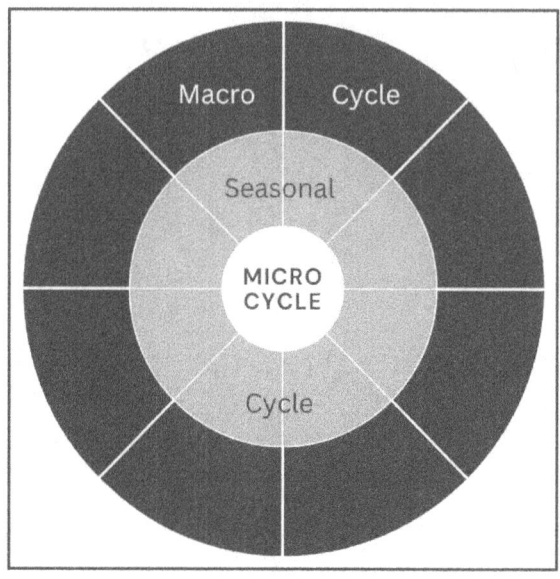

Image A

THE MYSTERY of our 7-year personal growth cycle is two-fold. Both the circle and the number 7 are cloaked in mystery and belong to the ancient world which is where our power as women also lies. For many of us, whilst we've heard of the 7- year life cycle, we know very little about it.

AT A QUANTUM LEVEL, it is fascinating to consider that we exist in a mathematical universe — one composed of numbers, patterns and the intricate relationships between them. In numerology, the number 7 is associated with mystery, spirituality and intuition. It represents depth, introspection and a quest for wisdom. We can compare this to number 4, which represents stability and 'the foundation of a matter'. In a tarot deck, the number 7 is the chariot card which means knowledge, self mastery and individual effort.

. . .

THE EARLY 20TH-CENTURY PHILOSOPHER, social reformer and mystic Rudolf Steiner integrated scientific and spiritual concepts outlining a life map based on 7-year cycles (each a period of transformation) and the 7 planets. For example our 1st personal growth cycle is influenced by the Moon (0-7 yrs), our 2nd by Mercury (7 to 14 yrs), 3rd by Venus (14 to 21 yrs), 4th by the Sun (21 to 28 yrs), 5th by Mars (28 to 35 yrs), 6th by Jupiter (35 to 42 yrs) and 7th by Saturn (42 to 49 yrs). We then move into the higher phases of influence, the 8th by the higher Moon (49 to 56 yrs), 9th by higher Mercury (56 to 63 yrs), 10th by higher Venus (63 to 70 yrs), 11th by the higher Sun (70 to 77 yrs), 12th by higher Mars (77 to 83 yrs), 13th by higher Jupiter (83-90) and 14th by higher Saturn (90 to 97).

THE NUMBER 7 also has much significance recurring in religious texts, nature, culture and art — take a moment to pause here and consider where it is that the number 7 appears.

THERE'S something undeniably powerful about the number 7. We live by 7 days in a week, the cycle that shapes our time. There are 7 deadly sins — and 7 heavenly virtues to counter them. Religion gives us 7 sacraments, and history celebrates the 7 wonders of the ancient world.

GAZE UP at the night sky and you'll find the 7 sisters of the Pleiades, woven into myth and star. The rainbow spans 7 vibrant colours, music flows through 7 distinct notes, and the Earth itself is divided into 7 continents, surrounded by 7 seas.

. . .

SO IT DOES MAKE you wonder — when it came to Snow White, why did she end up with 7 dwarfs? Not 5. Not 8. Why 7? Coincidence … or something more?

WE'VE all heard of the 7-year itch, also a classic Marilyn Monroe film — defining a common human experience when lots of relationships become stagnant and can break down. That is unless the relationship reaches a new and mutual level of maturity, wisdom and growth. The same can be said of nurturing the relationship within ourselves to reach a new level of wisdom, growth and maturity. It is our responsibility to do so, and this book is designed to help you achieve this.

BEING MYSTERIOUS, number 7 belongs to the ancient world and appears to signify 'more than the eye can see', it represents the 'unseen', or 'the veil' and for the Greeks it indicated absolute perfection or luck. For me and the purposes of our 7-year personal growth cycle it represents our spiritual journey, the journey of our soul and how it is that we will embody our spirit, wisdom and harness the opportunities and lessons of our individual personal growth journeys.

IN CHAPTER 6, we met the 7 main chakras plus the soul star chakra (*Image B*) to remind you of where we place them within The Genius Wheel® framework. As a reminder, the term chakra is a Sanskrit word meaning 'wheel' and refers to energy points or wheels within the body. They are thought to be spinning disks of energy that should stay open and aligned, as they correspond to the bundles of nerves, major organs, and areas of our energetic body that affect our emotional and physical wellbeing.

The Genius Wheel

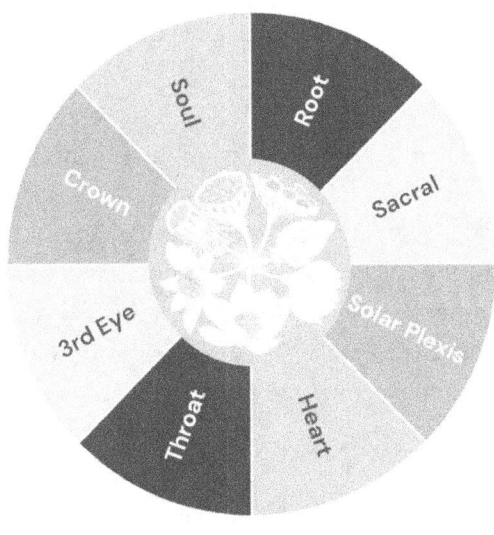

Image B

SCIENTISTS SAY we replace the cells in our bodies every 7 to 10 years — and in Traditional Chinese Medicine, a similar rhythm is recognised in women's lives through 7-year Qi cycles. These cycles are thought to shape key aspects of a woman's health, fertility, and overall life journey.

EACH 7-YEAR PHASE invites a different kind of nourishment and care, offering a powerful framework for women to understand and support their evolving health over time. This concept is outlined in *The Yellow Emperor's Inner Classic: Plain Questions*, an ancient text that details how each cycle brings about a new stage of development.

. . .

According to this view, a woman's life unfolds in distinct phases, each lasting 7 years, with noticeable physical, emotional, and energetic shifts occurring at the end of each cycle.

For example, the onset of menstruation (menarche) often occurs during the latter part of the 2nd personal growth cycle (ages 10 to 13) or the start of the 3rd personal growth cycle (ages 14 to 21). Fertility tends to peak in the following cycles and gradually declines between the 7th and 8th personal growth cycles (ages 42 to 55), aligning with the transition into menopause. These cycles continue into elderhood, marking deeper changes in vitality and spiritual focus.

We experience our most formative years within our 1st personal growth cycle — up to the age of 7. What happens here can inform the rest of our lives and it is here that many critical milestones are reached.

On average we have 10 to 12 personal growth cycles in our lifetime, as the UK average life expectancy is 80.7 years and worldwide it is 71.3 years old. You will recall in Chapter 2, you identified which personal growth cycle you were in and I've outlined how every 7 years we have a shift in our consciousness and awareness which is something we can in fact prepare for.

Previously we've mentioned either fear or dread over our *winter* phases but the reality is we don't get that many of them throughout our lifetime so wouldn't it be great if we used them wisely? Wouldn't it be great if we knew when to re-root ourselves and to see life not full of dead ends and glass ceilings but one where we can leverage the different phases that we find ourselves within?

. . .

THE MACRO CYCLE can help us to see the similar threads, patterns and opportunities and 'move through' them more purposefully and powerfully than in the last cycle. It is within this conversation that we can harness the power of our genius.

I HOPE you are ready to now dive into discovering how to work out your current phase and where you are within your own 7-year personal growth cycle? This is what we call our *macro* cycle.

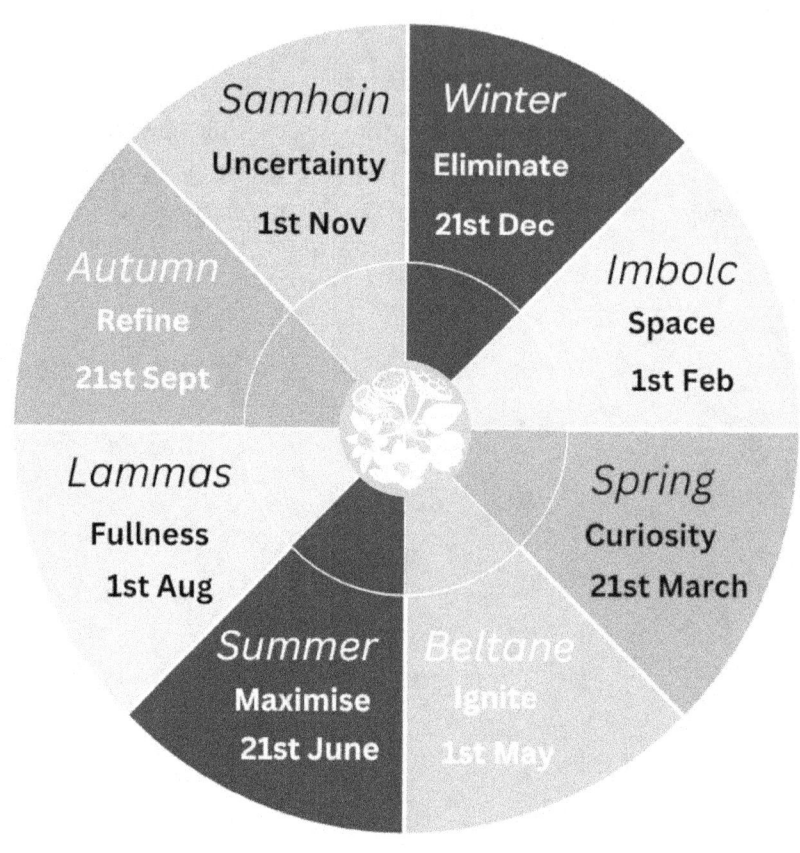

Image C

FINDING our starting point is one of the most challenging aspects of this work but once we've put the effort in to find it, we can use this as guidance for the rest of our lives. The guidance from this book, your intuition and reaching out to me via the Substack[1] community, or attending a retreat are all support mechanisms for you. Once you have an outline of your macro cycle, you can book a 1:1 intensive with me to explore it further. **ONE POWERFUL CALL.**[2] **A whole new chapter.**

ONCE WE NAIL down what phase you are currently in, you can start making sense of the past, understanding the now and even chart your course forward to the future.

THE GENIUS WHEEL® helps you understand how the 3 cycles — macro (outer circle), seasonal (middle circle), and micro (inner circle) — interact and function together as a unified whole. While we'll explore each cycle individually for clarity, it's important to remember that cycles are not linear, nor do they exist in isolation; each one exists within and influences the others. By breaking them down within The Genius Wheel® framework, we can better understand their unique roles and how they work in harmony.

---

1. luluminns.substack.com
2. thegeniuswheel.com/coaching

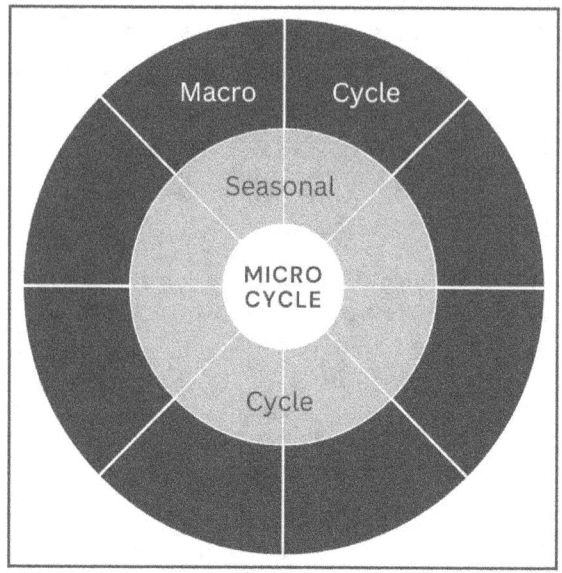

Image A

I ACTIVELY ENCOURAGE you to draw out your Genius Wheel circles, and I will show you in Chapter 10 exactly how you can use them for past, present and future growth.

7-year cycle — macro cycle (outer circle)
1-year cycle — seasonal cycle (middle circle)
29.5 day cycle — micro (inner circle)

OUR 7-YEAR CYCLE is longer than both the seasonal 12-month cycle (Chapter 6) and our micro (29.5-day) cycle (Chapter 8). The macro cycle holds both you and your personal growth journey as well as your micro cycle. We as women spend much of our time holding others, so it's great to know mother nature is holding you all of the time within one of her seasons — which when we bring conscious awareness to this, means you can leverage the energy of whichever phase of the cycle you currently find yourself within.

CHARTING your macro cycle with The Genius Wheel®

YOUR MACRO CYCLE is your 7-year personal growth cycle and apart from your lifetime cycle (and archetypes we met in Chapter 2), it will change the least frequently hence why it's called your macro (or large) cycle.

WITHIN THE MACRO CYCLE, each of the 8 seasons you met in Chapter 6 will appear and each will last for approximately 10.5 months or 21 months per season (remembering that each season has 2 parts or 2 phases).

IT'S important to remind you of the seasonal promise: the order of the 8 phases are always the same.

Remember:
Samhain belongs with *winter* (uncertainty and elimination)
Imbolc belongs with *spring* (space and curiosity)
Beltane belongs with *summer* (ignition and maximising)
Lammas belongs with *autumn* (fullness and refinement)

TO ENABLE you to find your current phase, I have broken this down into 3 simple steps on the next page.

. . .

TRUST THE PROCESS — it's messy and you will need to use your fingers to count or you can join The Genius Wheel® Substack to download the macro cycle spreadsheet.

STEP 1: Pick a significant *winter* moment in your life within the last 0 to 10 years.

REMEMBER *winter* is the energy of *uncertainty and elimination*. And usually involves a before and an after moment. There can be a period of uncertainty before it — i.e. should I leave this job, relationship or close this business? It may involve someone being unwell or the loss of someone or something. Sometimes it can even mean having a baby or starting a new relationship or marriage. But there is a clear before and after moment. Pick a *winter* moment and **trust you've picked it for a reason.**

AN OBVIOUS MOMENT for me was leaving my job as a lawyer (December 2014) and the period of *uncertainty* that preceded it. This is where I decided to start.

STEP 2: Once you've identified your *winter* moment, reflect on that time and work out a rough 2 years or 21 months when the season of *winter* held you. Then work out the seasons that followed for the same time period.

SEE MY EXAMPLE below and remember this is a draft.

. . .

June 2014 to Feb 2016 — *winter* (leaving my job Dec 2014)
  March 2016 to Nov 2017 — *spring*
  Dec 2017 - Aug 2019 — *summer*
  Sept 2019 - May 2021 — *autumn*
  June 2021 - Feb 2023 — *winter* (developed this framework)
  March 2023 — Nov 2024 — *spring*
  Dec 2024 — July 2026 — *summer*
  Aug 2026 — April 2028 — *autumn*
  May 2028 — Jan 2030 — *winter*

I went back 7 years and forward by 7 so I can plan my next cycle (exciting). Once you have your rough outline, you can move onto step 3.

Step 3: Create a table and add in the 4 x crossover phases

The next step is outlined below and will mean adding in the 4 crossover phases of *Imbolc, Beltane, Lammas* and *Samhain* (remember we spend 10.5 months in each of the 8 phases).

Be curious and see how specific with your timings you can get. There is lots of finger counting involved in this part, so please note this is not an easy process, you will tweak and add to it.

Remember to also have fun with it and trust that the process will be worth it.

Add notes in the right-hand column as to what was happening at the time of the season you think you were in

Date	Season	Notes
Feb 2014 to Dec 2014 Jan 2015 to **Oct 2015** **Winter**	Samhain - Uncertainty Winter - Eliminate	LEFT JOB AS LAWYER
Oct 2015 - Aug 2016 Sept 2016 to **July 2017** **Spring**	Imbolc - Space Spring - Curiosity	COACHING COURSE/1ST CLIENTS WROTE E-BOOK 5TH Personal Growth Cycle
July 2017 to May 2018 June 2018 to **April 2019** **Summer**	Beltane Ignite Summer Maximise	HOSTED MY 1ST RETREAT/BUSINESS BRANDING/COMMUNITY BUILDING
April 2019 to Feb 2020 March 2020 to **Nov 2020 Autumn**	Lammas Fullness Autumn - Refine	WANTED TO SELL MY HOUSE. MOVE TO CORNWALL
Nov 2020 to Sept 21 Oct 21 - **Sept 2022** **Winter**	Samhain - Uncertainty Winter - Eliminate	FINALLY SOLD HOUSE/FATHER EMERGENCY HEART SURGERY

IT IS ALSO normal to feel some apprehension about *winter* coming around next but we must remember the seasonal promise, *spring* always follows *winter* and it's a time for re-rooting and growth.

JUST LIKE YOUR personal growth cycle, The Genius Wheel® is ever evolving. Join us on Substack for updates, resources, toolkits and more.

8
YOUR MICRO CYCLE (THE 29.5-DAY CYCLE)

Your micro cycle is the smallest circle in the middle of your Genius Wheel and it represents the 29.5 day cycle that is either the moon or your menstrual cycle. This is the cycle that changes the most frequently as it's the shortest in length.

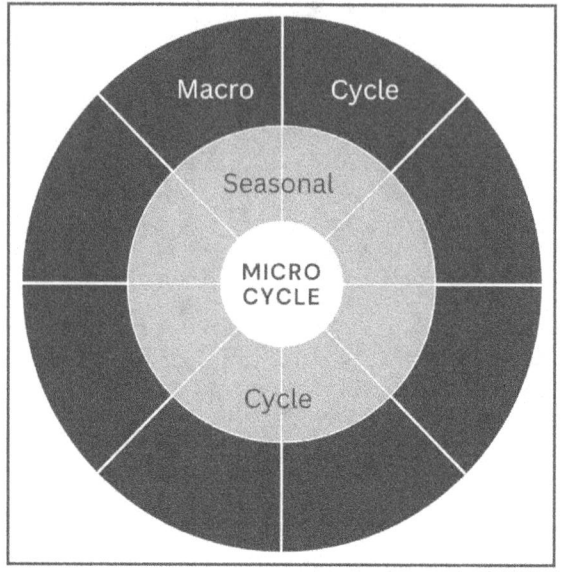

Image A

YOU CAN CHOOSE to follow either the moon cycle or, if it's still present, your menstrual cycle as your guide. Both the moon and the menstrual cycle wax and wane — expanding and contracting much like the seasons and the 7-year personal growth cycle — only on a more frequent rhythm.

ONE OF MY favourite childhood books was about a white cat and the moon — an old, well-thumbed copy with a battered silver cover that my mum had found in a charity shop. In the story, the cat is lost and believes that by following the moon, she'll find her way home. But as she journeys on, she comes to realise that the moon is always with her, no matter where she goes. I've always loved this as a metaphor for women — the moon, or *Grandmother Moon* as she's known by our Native American sisters, is mirrored in our menstrual cycle and offers a constant sense of home. Even after menopause, when our physical cycles begin to fade, the moon's rhythm continues to guide us, reminding us that its wisdom and cyclical presence remain within us always.

ON THAT NOTE, let me step away from the number 7 for a moment and turn to 13 — a number that has always resonated with me. Far from being unlucky, many of us as women feel quite the opposite and see it as a symbol of good fortune. This may be because, every 2 to 3 years, the moon completes 13 full cycles instead of 12. The additional full moon in such a year is known as a 'blue moon', giving rise to the saying 'once in a blue moon' — a phrase that hints at both rarity and a touch of magic. Similarly, some women experience 13 ovulations in a year rather than 12, which is often seen as a sign of strong energy — and, for those trying to conceive, a welcome opportunity. For all these reasons, I've come to see 13 as the 'goddess number' and Friday the 13th as 'goddess day'. Whether or not the patriarchy deliberately stigmatised the number 13, we can reclaim it — as a reminder of feminine power, lunar rhythm, and the enduring strength of the goddess within.

SO LET'S bring the luck of number 13 and start with the moon cycle which is a guide everyone can use for their Genius Wheel whether postmenopausal, on contraceptives, or having irregular bleeds — for many, the moon cycle and its impact is the preferred way to use the wheel.

THE MOON CYCLE:

THE MOON HAS a 29.5 day cycle with 8 distinct phases. These are the new moon, waxing crescent, 1st quarter, waxing gibbous, full moon, waning gibbous, 2nd quarter and waning crescent which are represented within The Genius Wheel® in the following image.

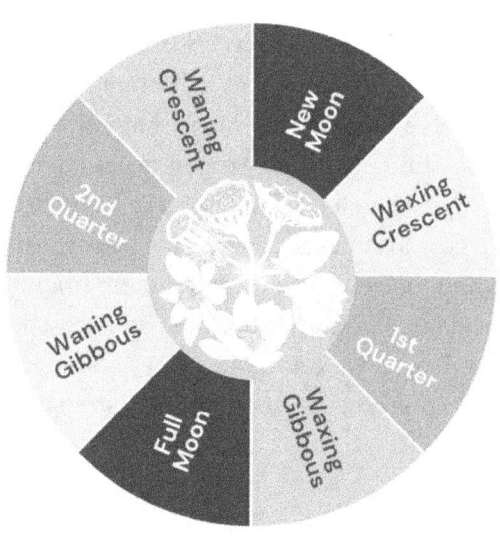

Image B

In Chapter 6, I took you through the seasonal cycle and how it corresponds to each of the 8 phases of the moon cycle.

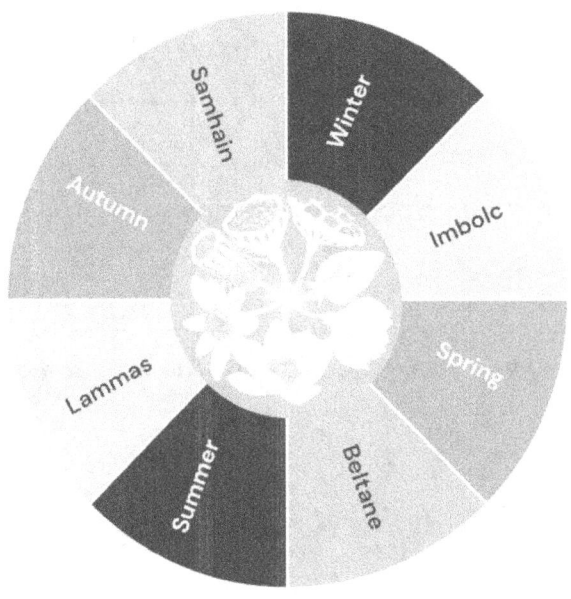

Image C

WINTER SOLSTICE CORRESPONDS with the new moon (and the energy of *elimination*).

IMBOLC CORRESPONDS with the waxing crescent moon (and the energy of *space*).

SPRING EQUINOX CORRESPONDS with the 1st quarter moon (and the energy of *curiosity*).

. . .

B*ELTANE* CORRESPONDS with the waxing gibbous moon (and the energy of *ignite*).

S*UMMER* S*OLSTICE* CORRESPONDS with the full moon (and the energy of *maximising*).

L*AMMAS* CORRESPONDS with the waning gibbous moon (and the energy of *fullness*).

A*UTUMN* E*QUINOX* CORRESPONDS with the 2nd quarter moon (and the energy of *refinement*).

S*AMHAIN* CORRESPONDS with the waning crescent moon (and the energy of *uncertainty*).

HERE **I** WILL HIGHLIGHT **how tracking the moon cycle can support us:**

W*HEN* I LEFT LEGAL PRACTICE — my macro cycle was *winter* — elimination. The season was also *Samhain* which means I had alignment in my decision of leaving my job, but the moon changes were interesting...

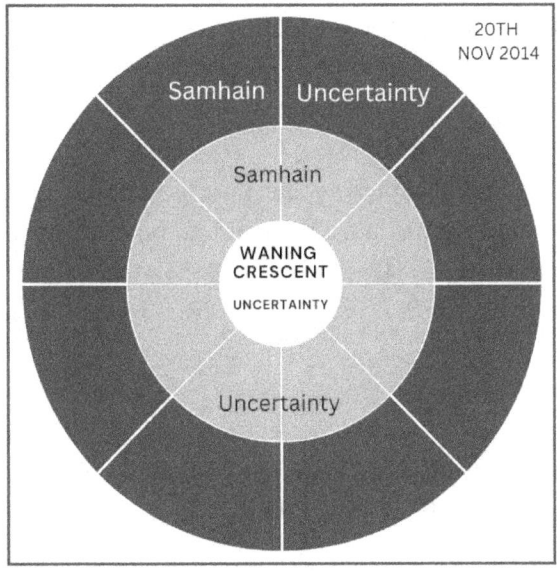

Image B

WHEN I MADE the decision to leave, it was 20th November 2014. The moon was in its waning crescent phase, which aligns with the energy of *Samhain* — a time of uncertainty. I felt deeply unsure about my choice and spent that weekend in New York, worried yet strangely aligned with the decision. The new moon — symbolic of *winter* and elimination — arrived on 22nd November. I returned to the office on 27th November and handed in my notice. I also informed the partners that, after 11 years of service, I would no longer attend any meetings with them. At that point, the moon had moved into its waxing crescent phase — associated with *Imbolc* and the energy of space — and I could feel myself beginning to step into something new. By 11th December, when I was placed on 'gardening leave', the moon was in its waning gibbous phase — connected to *Lammas* and fullness. The situation had reached its peak, and like the waning moon, I was ready to release it. I was also prepared to begin rediscovering who I was beyond that role. Over 10 years later, I created these Genius Wheels to reflect on the energies that were present during that powerful time of transition.

In Chapter 10, I will support you to complete your Genius Wheel for past, present and future dates. You can find both the past, present and future moon cycles on Google. I use SpaceWeatherLive[1] or LUNAF[2] — it is super fun to find out the moon cycle on the day you were born.

You can also purchase a Moonology diary by Yasmin Boland[3], or my preference is the beautiful annual moon cycle by Glitter Earth.[4]

The menstrual cycle:

On average a menstrual cycle is 29.5 days long but it can be much shorter or much longer. Like the moon and seasonal cycle, our menstrual cycle mirrors these cycles and also waxes and wanes in the same order. The dark or new moon (*winter*) represents our bleed (day 1). The full moon (*summer*) represents our ovulation/fertilisation (around day 14).

For many, early education about the menstrual cycle was severely lacking. We were taught little about our natural rhythm or our own fertility — only that we bleed and pregnancy must be avoided. It's fascinating, and frustrating, that women have long been given the

---

1. spaceweatherlive.com/en/moon-phases-calendar
2. lunaf.com
3. *Moonology, Working the Magic of the Lunar Cycles* by Yasmin Boland
4. https://www.glitterandearth.com/

sole responsibility for managing fertility, yet for generations, we were provided almost no real knowledge to support us in doing so. Only in relatively recent times have we begun to reclaim this understanding, deepening our connection to our bodies and cycles.

ANTHROPOLOGICAL STUDIES[5] even suggest men were forced away to hunt at the dark of the moon also the period of menstruation for women (enforcing a sex-strike), and then returned at the light of the full moon. Given the synchronisation that could happen in a community of close-knit women and connection to the moon cycle, this indicated men returned at the time of ovulation. During this time our ancestors were much more in tune with and guided by the cycles of nature.

THERE IS 'NO NORMAL' menstrual cycle and many of us have a different sitting point as to the length and our experience of it. Menstruation is far from a linear process particularly in the modern world and disruption of our circadian rhythms. I've been tracking my own cycle for 7 years and it tends to sit between 26 to 28 days, and I most comfortably menstruate around the new moon. I was in the *spring* phase of my 6th personal growth cycle when I decided to come off the pill and track my cycle. Shortly after I came across the work of *Red School*.

RED SCHOOL and the authors of *Wild Power*,[6] Alexandra Pope and Sjanie Hugo Wurlitzer, are pioneers of seeing both our menstruality and menstrual awareness as being part of an essential spiritual practice. A practice which is capable of unleashing our wild feminine

---

5. Chris Knight, Blood Relations: Menstruation and the Origins of Culture
6. *Wild Power,* Discover the Magic of your Menstrual Cycle by Alexandra Pope and Sjanie Hugo

power whilst linking each phase of the menstrual cycle with the seasons of *spring, summer, autumn and winter.*

THEY APPEARED on the launch series of She Rebel Radio® in 2019[7]:

"WE TALK *about the menstrual cycle as having these inner seasons. And so menstruation is what we call the inner winter. That's a time when you kind of want to retreat and go in and do nothing.*

AND YOUR PRE-OVULATORY *time is your inner spring. And the ovulatory time is the inner summer.*

AND THE PRE-MENSTRUAL TIME, *we call the inner autumn. The tone, energy and feel of the seasons change. The spring energy is that lovely energy of growth and into the summer energy, which is really superwoman territory, where we can be all things to all people.*

AND THEN IN *the second half of the cycle, we feel ourselves being drawn into greater complexity and sensitivity with ourselves and then there's that moment where at the end of our premenstrual time is the inner autumn where we want to pull away from the world and stop at menstruation."*

Alexandra Pope and Sjanie Hugo Wurlitzer

A TYPICAL 28 to 29-day cycle might look like this:

---

7. She Rebel Radio®, Episode 8 https://sites.libsyn.com/210074/unleashing-your-wild-feminine-power

Period	Season	Days/Notes
Menstruation (bleed)	**WINTER into** *Imbolc* (Elimination & Space)	1 to 7
Preovulation	**SPRING into** *Beltane* (Curiosity & Ignite)	7 to 14
Ovulation (fertility)	**SUMMER into** *Lammas* (Maximise & Fullness)	14 to 21
Premenstrual	**AUTUMN into** *Samhain* (Refine & Uncertainty)	21 to 28

RED SCHOOL[8] name day 21 or thereabouts as being of particular significance as 'the call to the temple' when our world goes from being outward facing to more inward facing. Whilst tracking my cycle, I began to notice a rise in anxiety around social events, on or around day 21 and the crossover day, where I felt the call to attend to my inner terrain. We can think of the *autumn* phase of our macro cycle as having a similar switchover.

I ALSO LIKE the ancient theory as documented in *Red Moon* by Miranda Gray[9], where she stated a red moon woman is one who menstruates around the full moon and embodies the characteristics

---

8. Red School, https://www.redschool.net/
9. *Red Moon, Understanding and Using the Creative, Sexual and Spiritual gifts of the Menstrual Cycle* by Miranda Gray

of a healer, shaman or priestess — a spiritual teacher of sorts and is likely to be the women most marginalised by society. The woman who menstruates around the new or dark moon (i.e. when she is supposed to), is a white moon woman who is said to embody the mother archetype and nurturing energy of the mother.

CHARTING THE MICRO CYCLE:

OUR MICRO CYCLE is the moon or our menstrual cycle which is the cycle which changes seasons the most frequently and consistently. The cycle of the moon is the easiest, most inclusive and makes lots of impact for women. It is easier to also chart back and forward with.

HERE I WILL SHOW you how you can fit your menstrual cycle or the moon cycle into the 8 phases of The Genius Wheel®.

STEP 1: Work out the average length of your menstrual cycle or use the moon 29.5 cycle

IF YOU DON'T PRESENTLY HAVE a cycle or it's very erratic due to perimenopause/menopause or the pill — you can use the moon cycle which is 29.5 days.

THOSE OF YOU who have a menstrual cycle of 25 to 31 days will always have a crossover day on day 4. If you have a cycle of 33 to 39 days, you will have a crossover day at day 5.

. . .

IF YOUR CYCLE is 24 or 32 days, there are no crossover days and this may be a smoother transition.

STEP 2: Use this table or create your own for a longer or shorter cycles

Days	Divided by 8	Days per phase
24 days	No crossover day	3 days
25 to 27 days	Crossover on day 4, 11, 18 and 25	3.1 - 3.3
28 days	Crossover on day 4, 11, 18 and 25	3.5 days
29 to 31 days	Crossover on day 4, 11, 18 and 25	3.6 to 3.8
33 to 39 days	Crossover on day 5, 12, 19 and 26	4.1 to 4.8
32 or 40 days	No crossover day	4 or 5 days

ON THE FOLLOWING pages is a 28-day cycle or moon cycle (you can use this for anything between a 25 to 31 day cycle).

Appendix C : Example of Menstrual Cycle with 8 phases

Day	Phase (Mini Cycle)	Energy	Notes	Personal Notes
1	Winter (1st day of bleed) New moon Root chakra	Eliminate	Reducing or removing something by choice or not. Loss, confusion or grief. Liberation, ease and relief.	
2	Winter	Eliminate		
3	Winter	Eliminate		
4	**Winter/Imbolc Crossover day**	**Eliminate/ Space**	Openness/roominess Sense of freedom, unburdened, free and at ease.	
5	Imbolc Waxing crescent Sacral chakra	Space		
6	Imbolc	Space		
7	Imbolc	Space		
8	Spring 1st quarter Solar plexus chakra	Curiosity	Exploring and seeking out opportunities. Enjoyment of learning new things and keen interest	
9	Spring	Curiosity		
10	Spring	Curiosity		
11	**Spring/Beltane Crossover day**	**Curiosity/ ignite**		
12	Beltane	Ignite	Strong passion, enthusiasm, or	

	Waxing gibbous Heart chakra		inspiration. Feeling intense enjoyment, to breath life into	
13	*Beltane*	Ignite		
14	*Beltane*	Ignite		
15	*Summer* Full moon Throat chakra	Maximise	To increase something as much as possible.	
16	*Summer*	Maximise	Push, expand and grow, reach potential.	
17	*Summer*			
18	**Summer /Lammas** **Crossover day**	**Maximise/ fullness**		
19	*Lammas* Waning gibbous 3rd Eye chakra	Fullness	Fulfilment of destiny, reap the rewards. Enjoy the good things that come. Feeling of satisfaction contentment and progress	
20	*Lammas*	Fullness		
21	*Lammas*	Fullness/ refine		
22	*Autumn* Final quarter Crown chakra	Refine	Level of discernment and preference	
23	*Autumn*	Refine	Judging without judgement. Discretion.	
24	*Autumn*	Refine	What is the wisdom I've gained?	

25	*Autumn/ Samhain* **Crossover Day**	**Refine/ uncertainty**		
26	*Samhain* Waning crescent Soul star chakra	Uncertainty	Unease and inability to make plans.	
27	*Samhain*	Uncertainty	What am I certain and uncertain about?	
28	*Samhain*	Uncertainty		

. . .

NOTE: The 4 crossover days are when one phase meets another — *winter* into *Imbolc, Spring* into *Beltane, Summer* into *Lammas, Autumn* into *Samhain* — as it's a shift of energy of earth into air, air into fire, fire into water, water into earth.

YOUR CROSSOVER DAYS may be different or not matter to you. That is because:

SAMHAIN BELONGS with *winter* (uncertainty and elimination)

IMBOLC BELONGS with *spring* (space and curiosity)

BELTANE BELONGS with *summer* (ignition and maximising)

LAMMAS BELONGS with *autumn* (fullness and refinement)

STEP 3: You can use the above table as the smallest circle in your Genius Wheel.

A GREAT PRACTICE is to use the guide above to work out what energy your menstrual cycle is in today.

I.E. TODAY I am on day 8 (of my 26 to 28 day cycle) — so this is a crossover day for me into *spring*: *curiosity*.

. . .

Just like the 29.5 day cycle, The Genius Wheel® is ever evolving — join us on Substack[10] for updates, resources, toolkits and more.

IN THE NEXT CHAPTER, we will discover the power of ritual and (how) it can deepen your connection with your 7-year personal growth cycle.

---

10. luluminns.substack.com

9

THE POWER OF RITUAL

"We live in a world that values the rational mind, and has forgotten the sacred gift."
ALBERT EINSTEIN

In this chapter, we explore the power of ritual and how it can help us connect with the unfolding of our genius throughout our 7-year personal growth cycle. It's our conversation with the elements that unfolds our genius, and we can use rituals to help us.

MARKING seasonal shifts is an ancient ritual, deeply rooted in our ancestors' connection to nature, as their survival depended on understanding and adapting to the changing seasons. They were also far more comfortable with what they didn't know and understand, yet today, we allow our rational mind to get in the way of what is magical about life.

. . .

While modern life has distanced us from these rhythms, acknowledging seasonal transitions can not only help us realign with nature, our well-being (for rest and renewal), and the cycles of growth — we've discovered it helps us connect with our 7-year personal growth cycle. Rituals are essential in marking the crossovers and transitions we have within the cycle.

What is a ritual?

A ritual is a way of behaving or a series of actions which people regularly carry out in a particular situation, because it is their custom to do so. A ritual needs to include *an action or the actual doing of something*, whilst words can be included there must be more than that. In order to bring power to a ritual, we must also add in two important ingredients: firstly, it must engage the senses and secondly, there must be a strong reason or intention behind it.

Engaging our senses allows connection to our subconscious mind and the reptilian brain which is more sensory — this in turn connects us to a much greater field of intelligence increasing both creativity and flow in our lives.

Rituals can be just one action, such as burning a story or belief you no longer wish to have but most often we recognise them as traditionally repeated on particular dates, occasions or times.

The clink of a glass to celebrate births, birthdays, christmas, graduations, weddings and funerals are times that many of us engage in rituals without even thinking about it. We often have lots of personalised rituals we engage in with our families; my mum always buys us a birthday card from the cats. At Christmas, we used to always listen to Elvis and open our presents strictly after lunch, which is deemed a weird ritual by many. Yet rituals within our own families enable us to foster a sense of connection and belonging with one another.

RITUALS ALSO BECOME OUTDATED — growing up, the birthday bumps were the norm but are no longer something deemed nice or safe for children. We also stopped listening to Elvis sometime after my Grandmother passed away but it's a time I always remember fondly. A funeral or the anniversary of someone's death is when we may take flowers to a place of significance, listen to their favourite song or meet loved ones to honour the memories of the person we love. This creates connection.

SPORTS PROFESSIONALS, musicians and other performers often have rituals and things they do before going out onto the pitch or onto stage which has been shown to improve their performance, increase confidence and also the bonding of a team or group.

ON A SMALLER SCALE, many of us have rituals we engage in throughout the cycle of our day. Perhaps something we do when we first get up or finish the day — we may meditate, read or write. Some may jump in the shower or even light a cigarette. When we get home from work or the office, we may change our clothes or pour ourselves a drink before dinner.

BUT WHAT WOULD LIFE, business and our relationships look like if we created more intentional rituals for ourselves? Many of the rituals shared above are really marking a change, transition or crossover point within our lives. Birth, death, marriage. Daytime to nighttime.

The transition from work to home. Who we are before a performance to who we become when the performance itself happens. As women, we tend to have even more roles, transitions and phases — what would our lives look like if with intention we used rituals to mark the shifts we experience?

TRADITIONALLY, anthropologists and social scientists considered the impact of rituals upon us as both ancient and modern communities and societies. But there is now an increasing amount of work by psychologists to consider the impact of ritual upon our wellbeing, personal performance, resilience and even our identity.

HARVARD PROFESSOR, Francesca Gino and Michael Norton,[1] a renowned Harvard psychologist, have both studied the use of rituals and confirmed the following benefits [2]:

1. Bringing a sense of control at a time of loss or uncertainty.
2. Deepening our enjoyment, connection and bonding with one another.
3. Increasing our confidence, maximising our effort and powerfully increasing performance.

RITUALS CAN ALSO ADD MORE purpose and pleasure to our lives and can turn even the most mundane moments into meaningful ones. In fact, Norton goes so far as to say that whilst our habits automate behaviour, it is our rituals which animate and turn what may be

---

1. *The Ritual Effect*, The Transformative Power of Our Everyday Actions by Michael Norton
2. https://hbr.org/2020/04/the-restorative-power-of-ritual

boring and lacklustre into a vast technicolour. We can distinguish, habits being 'what we do' to rituals being 'how we do' them — the more idiosyncratic they are, the more meaning they will hold.

WITHOUT A RITUAL to orient ourselves we can feel lost and become lost in between identities, Norton highlights that rituals mark extremely significant life transitions, helping us to take ownership of our next phase. They act as a bridge from the past to the future and help us to see ourselves anew.

DURING A RETREAT WITH ME — one client Tessa, discovered she'd been lost in the *summer*/go-getter phase of her life. As such, since she'd left the corporate world and become a grandmother she'd remained stuck hankering for her old life and stepping in on her daughter's parenting. She now realised she needed to step back and embrace her *autumn*/genius phase! It was a huge transitional moment, and we marked the retreat with many rituals throughout the weekend. Tessa left feeling excited to embrace this phase of her life, commenting that her husband would also be happy she was finally ready to embrace it.

THE 7-YEAR personal growth cycle by way of The Genius Wheel® — along with the use of rituals to mark the transitory and crossover moments to orient ourselves — in turn enables us to bring more wisdom, growth and maturity to each phase. Creating these rituals reminds us that there is no hierarchy within a cycle, and no phase is better than the other.

THE OVERALL SHIFT we are making throughout our 7-year personal growth cycle (which repeats) is a transition from the heavier and slower energy (of water and earth/*autumn* and *winter*) into the lighter and quicker energy (of air and fire/*spring* and *summer*).

USING RITUALS, we can begin to honour them all equally which is why becoming part of The Genius Wheel® Substack[3] community is an important way for us as women to gather together to mark each season, and our belonging within them at any particular moment in time.

ANOTHER IMPORTANT STEP is to grab your calendar and mark the month of your next transitory or crossover moment from your *macro cycle* from one phase into the other. Notice the shifts you are feeling and find a way to mark it. I will share with you a ritual on the next page.

---

3. luluminns.substack.com

RITUAL for your crossover or transitory phase:

1. Mark your crossover/transition from one phase of your *macro cycle* into the other in your diary. This will be the month you are transitioning or crossing over.
2. Nearer the time — pick a day you'd like to conduct a ritual to mark this transition or crossover.
3. Make sure you have space and can be alone for your ritual.
4. Write down the new phase you are entering into and the relevant phrase :

- I welcome you *'winter'* and the energy of elimination into my life. I will boldly eliminate what is no longer serving me. I will step into the void.
- I welcome you *'Imbolc'* and the energy of space into my life. I will immerse myself in the new space and see what emerges.
- I welcome you *'spring'* and the energy of curiosity into my life. I will be curious and enjoy all that my curiosity brings to me.
- I welcome you *'Beltane'* and all the igniting energy into my life. I will choose wisely that which I wish to ignite.
- I welcome you *'summer'* and all the energy of maximising my life. I will expand, reach and grow.
- I welcome you *'Lammas'* and the energy of fullness into my life. I celebrate the abundance and slowly welcome beginning to turn inwards.
- I welcome you *'autumn'* and the energy of refinement into my life. I will distill the lessons and remember to keep the most important parts.
- I welcome you *'Samhain'* and the energy of uncertainty into my life. I will find peace in learning what I can and cannot control.

5. Light a candle as you say the words out loud for the *macro* cycle you are welcoming in.
6. Allow yourself 30 minutes to write down some intentions for this phase.
7. Write down anything that will not be coming with you into this next phase. If you'd like too, let go of the previous phase and perhaps burn anything that needs releasing.
8. Place an item of significance and with intention in the corresponding direction for your macro cycle within your home i.e. *Winter* is north, *Imbolc* is north east, *spring* is east, *Beltane* is south east, *summer* is south, *Lammas* is south west, *autumn* is *west*, *Samhain* is north west. It may be the candle you have been using, a bunch of flowers, a plant or a special personal item. You might change a picture on the wall to something of more relevance for this phase. You might be inspired perhaps by what is already in the space now.
9. As you blow your candle out, say a thank you to your personal growth cycle for holding you for the next 10.5 months: "I'm grateful for the lessons of this phase and its place within my cycle. I thank you *Samhain/winter, Imbolc/spring, Beltane/summer, Lammas/autumn* for all the lessons and growth you shall bring and for holding space for me. I honour you and all the other seasons within my cycle."

IN THE FINAL CHAPTER, I share with you 10 ways you can use your Genius Wheel for the past, the present and the future.

10

USING YOUR GENIUS WHEEL

The Genius Wheel® is designed to help you orientate yourself within your 7-year personal growth cycle which before now has been undefined and unchartered territory. You can use The Genius Wheel® to reflect on your cycle of growth, healing and empowerment to gain clarity over your current phase but also to identify how you can leverage the energy of your future phases.

THE FRAMEWORK HELPS us to understand that our growth, healing and empowerment really does happen in phases, cycles and patterns. By integrating our lessons rather than leaving them fragmented, we gain clarity and ease in navigating each phase. As The Genius Wheel® deepens our conscious awareness, the seeds we sow become richer, and the lessons we harvest grow even more powerful.

WHEN USED CORRECTLY, The Genius Wheel® can be seen as a way of life. One that is cyclical and not linear as we commit to unleashing more of our genius along the way. We can begin to make sense of our life's journey and how the seasons have held and supported us throughout. The first step is to always work out what our *macro cycle* is, as I shared with you in Chapter 7.

In this chapter, I'll share 10 powerful ways you can work with your Genius Wheel — assuming you've already identified your *macro cycle*.

This chapter will be divided into 3 parts:

1. How you can use your Genius Wheel for the present moment
2. How you can use your Genius Wheel to understand the past
3. How you can use your Genius Wheel to plan for the future

Once you have your *macro cycle* as per Chapter 7, let's begin to explore the 10 practical ways you can use your Genius Wheel:

1. Use the Seasonal Cycle:

One of the simplest ways to use your Genius Wheel is by focusing on the seasonal cycle, that is the middle circle on your Genius Wheel. Over 12 months — each of the 8 phases lasts for 6 weeks — you can pull cards and undertake significant rituals and activities.

It is incredibly important to tune in, with and experience, the energy of each of the 8 phases of the seasonal cycle as this is how we begin to understand and experience more deeply how these phases show up within our 7-year personal growth cycle as well as what they mean to us personally. So let's get started!

Steps:

1. Mark the points for each of 8 phases of the seasonal cycle in your diary and you may wish to re-read the relevant section in Chapter 7. As a reminder for the Northern Hemisphere these dates are: 1st February (*Imbolc*), 21st March (*Spring Equinox*), 1st May (*Beltane*), 21st June (*Summer Solstice*), 1st August (*Lammas*), 21st September (*Autumn Equinox*), the 1st Nov (*Samhain*), 21st December (*Winter Solstice*). Please note each marker takes place over a few days or may shift a day or two but the above is the easiest way to remember when they are, which is every 6 weeks (on either the 1st or the 21st).

2. For the Southern Hemisphere, you'll need to swap each date to its polar opposite and twin — remember the polarity principle in Chapter 4.

3. You can conduct your own ritual on the above dates by sitting in meditation, pulling an oracle card or journaling on each of the energies as I've outlined in Chapter 7. You may wish to place something in your home or garden in the correct direction, i.e. if it's the *Summer Solstice*, towards the south or the *Autumn Equinox*, towards the west.

4. If you'd like to join others in marking the seasons by way of meditation, journaling and oracle cards — I'd love to invite you to join us within the Substack[1] community.

5. You might also attend a seasonal yoga class or download a meditation from YouTube relevant to the season.

2. Chart your Course Today:

THE SECOND STEP of your Genius Wheel is charting your course today or within this next week. You will mark your *macro cycle*, the *seasonal cycle* and the *micro cycle* if you wish to add it in.

---

1. luluminns.substack.com

The Genius Wheel

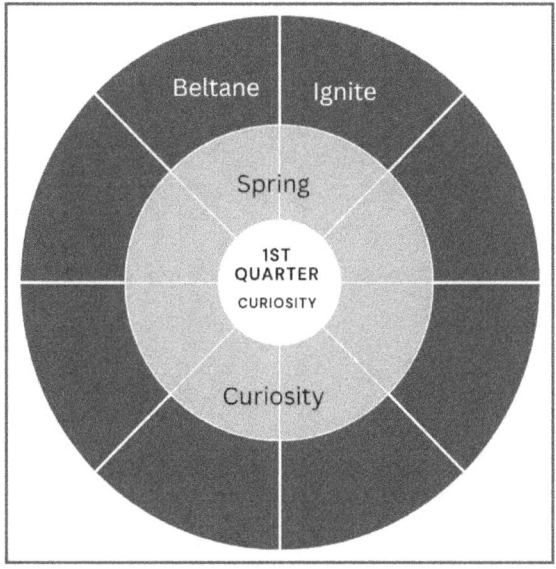

Image A

STEPS:

1. **Remind yourself of your macro cycle** (Chapter 7) for the year ahead - the largest circle and mark this on the wheel as above.

In the example on the previous page (*Image A*), I have used my macro phase of *Beltane* (ignite) from June 2024 to April 2025 which I have marked on the largest circle.

2. **Identify the seasonal cycle** (Chapter 6) we are in today plus the energy that goes with this phase, mark this within the middle circle. As a reminder these dates are the 1st Nov (*Samhain*), 21st December (*Winter Solstice*), 1st Feb (*Imbolc*), 21st March (*Spring Equinox*), 1st May (*Beltane*), 21st

June (*Summer Solstice*), 1st August (*Lammas*), 21st September (*Autumn Equinox*).

3. **Identify your micro cycle** (Chapter 8) - you can use today's moon phase or work out your menstrual cycle or both. Mark this in the smallest circle.
4. If you wish, you can pull an oracle card for an insight into a question that you may have about today or this week coming up?

3. Check your Alignment Positions:

AT VARIOUS TIMES within your Genius Wheel, you will have alignment positions which you can harness the power of. Alignment positions are when they are in the same phase and in agreement with each other which means we can supercharge the energy.

FOR EXAMPLE, your *macro* and *seasonal cycle* are often in the same phase for up to a 6 week period. Remember your *micro cycle* changes the most frequently which means there will be periods of a few days where it is aligned with either your *macro cycle* and/or the *seasonal cycle*. It gets really exciting when all 3 are in alignment with one another and depending on the energy ie. if it's *winter*, you can super charge *elimination* or *summer,* you can super charge the energy of *maximising*. Remember cycles do not have hierarchy — all the seasons are valued and respected in the same way remembering that one cannot exist without the other.

I VIVIDLY REMEMBER the moment I decided to leave my job as a lawyer — it was 20th November 2014, the day I flew out on holiday to New York. This was several years before I created *The Genius Wheel®*. While writing this book and reflecting on that period, I was struck by the realisation that all 3 cycles were in *Samhain*, aligned in a powerful way with the energy of *uncertainty*. The synchronicity was incredible.

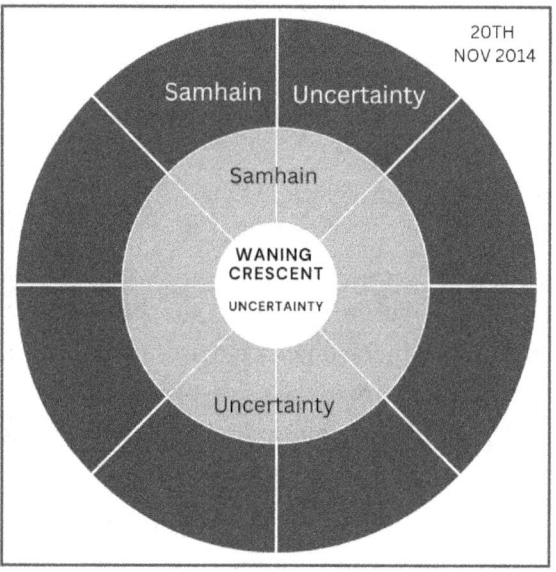

Image B

STEPS:

1. Using your Genius Wheel completed in exercise 2, **check whether any of your 3 cycles** are in alignment (2 match) or super alignment (3 match).

2. **Remember** it is more than normal for your cycles to not be in alignment which is why it's great when we find alignment! I will share with you a little later how you can chart your course forward and find your alignment positions in the future.

3. **If there is alignment between 2 or 3 of the cycles**
   — maybe pick an activity that serves the energy you are in.

WHAT ACTIVITIES COULD ALIGN with your day or the remainder of the season? I.e. *Imbolc* (space), go back to Chapter 6 and read that section.

4. **Align your Annual Intentions or Goals with your Macro Cycle:**

ONE OF THE most important aspects of The Genius Wheel® is to ensure that your annual intentions or goals align with the energy of your *macro cycle* for the year ahead! You will feel more in the natural flow of your goals for the year as opposed to going against the grain and doing the opposite of the energy you are in.

MOST PEOPLE FORCE and push themselves at the wrong time, which is where burnout, overwhelm and overthinking come in. Being in your inner *winter* gives you permission to pause and to stop forcing clarity to come in. This ensures better energy in your *spring* and *summer* and avoids disappointment about unmet goals and expectations for the year ahead. Relax instead and be in flow. If you are in *Beltane* or *summer — get clear about what you are igniting and maximising.* Use the time to get focused. Or if in *spring* — allow yourself to open up and explore. *Autumn* requires maturity and refining carefully.

HONOUR THE CONTRACTED phases and enjoy the expansive ones. Remember contraction is the key expansion and the secret to creating better balance in our lives. It is game changing to match our intentions with our personal growth cycle.

Steps:

1. Remind yourself of your macro cycle as per Chapter 7 and mark off any crossover points for the year. I.e. Are you moving from *Spring Equinox* (curiosity) into *Beltane* (ignite) this year?

2. Journal what that means for your annual intentions or goals? Read the relevant sections to your macro cycle in Chapter 7 and reflect.

3. Check your annual intentions and goals align with the energy you will be in? Can you ramp it up for the 2nd half of the year or should you be scaling it back? I.e. *Lammas* (fullness) into *autumn* (refinement).

If you're ready to gain clarity on what your cycle means and how it aligns with your goals and intentions, I invite you to book a **75-minute deep-dive session**[2] with me. This is where we go beyond the surface — unpacking your unique cycle, identifying what's holding you back, and creating an intentional path forward.

Join me on Substack for ongoing insights, or if you're feeling called to real transformation, **book your 75-minute session now and let's begin the shift together.**

5. Work with the Chakra and/or Element of your Macro Cycle:

---

[2] thegeniuswheel.com/coaching

ONCE YOU'VE IDENTIFIED your *macro cycle* and any crossover points, one of the most embodied ways you can use your Genius Wheel is by identifying the corresponding chakra.

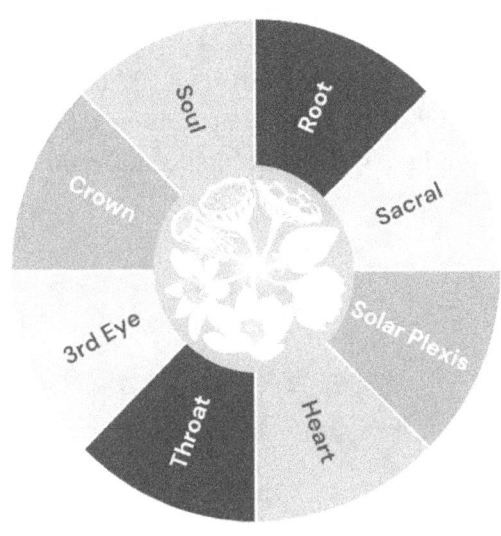

Image C

AS A REMINDER, a chakra is a Sanskrit word meaning wheels of energy within the body. When we open up the wheels in the body, we create more alignment and flow within our lives. One of the reasons I used the chakras within The Genius Wheel® is because I'd noticed quite naturally since my yoga practice that every 7 years, I'd been working through them quite methodically from the root chakra all the way up to crown. I then found myself back at the root chakra again.

. . .

ONE OF MY best-selling 1:1 coaching courses, *The 3 Keys to Self-Actualisation,* corresponds each key to a particular chakra and alignment within the body. As Sharon Blackie on She Rebel Radio® commented, "Women have a slower and more embodied wisdom." I've found by working with women for the past 10 years, that when we can find a corresponding position within the body for personal development work, it holds a much greater significance for us. In addition to which, we have emotional blockages within the body and pioneers such as Peter Levine[3] and Bessel van der Kolk[4] have achieved a significant amount of work to show that trauma (and stuckness) lives within the body and not within our intellectual mind.

---

3. *Waking the Tiger:* Healing Trauma by Peter Levine
4. *The Body Keeps a Score: Brain,* Mind and Body in the Healing of Trauma by Bessel Van der Kolk

STEPS:

1. **Identify your chakra**

Using the tables below you can re-identify your *macro cycle* for the year and locate the corresponding chakra.

Season	Chakra	Colour	Element
Winter	**Root chakra - bottom of the spine**	Red	Earth
Imbolc	**Sacral chakra - below belly button**	Orange	Earth/air
Spring	**Solar plexus - above belly button**	Yellow	Air
Beltane	**Heart chakra**	Green/Pink	Air/fire

Summer	**Throat chakra**	Blue	Fire
Lammas	**Third eye -in between & above eyes**	Indigo	Fire/water
Autumn	**Crown - top of head**	Violet/white	Water
Samhain	**Soul star chakra - above head**	White	Water/earth

2. **Take it with you to your yoga class or find meditations on YouTube**

ONCE YOU HAVE IDENTIFIED your corresponding chakra, you can take that chakra with you to your yoga class. If your teacher has a focus on the chakras or some of them, you'll know which one is of particular significance to you as it relates to your *macro cycle*. If your mind wanders during yoga, you can bring it back to focusing your intention on the chakra which is relevant to you right now.

3. Identify the colour or element for your corresponding chakra

EACH OF THE chakras have a corresponding colour which you can see within the table above. You may want to consider how you can bring more of that colour into your life for this phase of your macro cycle?

EXAMPLE: When I was in my *spring* phase (curiosity) — I suddenly developed a fondness for yellow which I've not had since the age of 11! Perhaps it was the influence of my *spring* phase. I brought a yellow jumper, outdoor rug, matching beanbag and some yellow blankets.

4. Advanced step

YOU MAY ALSO WISH to identify the corresponding element using the table on the previous pages.

THE MAIN SEASONS have one element: *spring* (air), *summer* (fire), *autumn* (water) and *winter* (earth).

IF YOUR MACRO *cycle* is in one of the main seasons, you may wish to climb a mountain (air), attend a fire ceremony or burn some old beliefs (fire), visit a waterfall or go wild swimming (water) or walk barefoot in the forest (earth).

THE CROSSOVER SEASONS have a mixture of elements: *Imbolc* (earth/air), *Beltane* (air/fire), *Lammas* (fire/water) and *Samhain* (water/earth) - these are quite important balancing energies.

. . .

For *Imbolc*, as you move into air it keeps you grounded. For *Beltane*, the oxygen of air ignites and energises the fires. For *Lammas*, water following the fire starts to cool it all down. For *Samhain*, water on earth creates hydration. Ask the question, how might you work with both of these energies together?

IF YOU ARE a member of The Genius Wheel® Substack community, you will receive journaling tools and a group meditation every 6 weeks where we use both the chakra, element and positioning of the season to ensure you have an embodied experience throughout the year.

6. Chart Back your Course:

LOOKING BACK to the past is one of my favourite ways of using The Genius Wheel®. We can check our *macro cycle* and pull out a message from the past that we may have missed at the time or when things were particularly difficult.

FOR EXAMPLE, it could be a challenging period in your business or career, the end of a relationship, a serious health issue affecting you or a loved one, selling your home, or making difficult financial or purchasing decisions.

DURING THE LOCKDOWN YEARS, I was trying to sell my house for 2 years and had a total of 5 buyers! It was hell. Eventually, in September 2022 the sale finally went through. Upon creating my Genius Wheel for this time — I noticed two significant things. Firstly, the month the house sold was a crossover month for me where I left the *winter* phase of *elimination* and moved into *Imbolc* (space). If I'd known this beforehand, it would have given me a good indication of where I was at and not to push the sale earlier. Secondly, when I pulled an oracle card upon the cycle — the message was clear — *be gentle, be patient*. I'd been doing the opposite and using a lot of push/force energy.

I CREATED my Genius Wheel for the following phase and on a date that my father was taken to hospital in an ambulance. The card I pulled was 'sacred one' with an old man in the picture. He is sacred to me and luckily for me, I had the space and time to be with him as much as possible when he needed me to be. Had my house sale gone through earlier, I might not have been local to where he lived but the delays had changed everything so I was exactly where I needed to be.

IT HELPED me make sense of my path — that there is always a higher plan that is way beyond what I might think needs to happen. The same is true for all of us.

MAKING sense of what we may or may not have missed from our past helps us to have faith in our orientation in the here and now. It can prevent us from repeating similar patterns of behaviour and mistakes. It helps us to build trust and rapport with our personal growth cycles, reminding us it's never too late to learn a lesson or bring greater conscious awareness to something from the past. By doing so, we can actually change the future. When we have the ability to see something bigger than ourselves, a wider perspective — we have the chance to re-orientate ourselves in the present moment.

Steps:

1. **Pick a challenging moment of your past**

This may be from one of your previous *winter* moments and similar to the moments I've shared in this chapter. You might have been reminded of many of these moments when reflecting on your past cycles and in locating your *macro cycle*. It might be a past moment that you feel is still keeping you stuck in some way.

2. **Write down the date**

Write the date of the past event onto a piece of paper — if you want to add your micro cycle, you'll need an exact date but otherwise the month and year is enough.

3. **Create your Genius Wheel**

Underneath, create your Genius Wheel with the 3 circles — including your *macro cycle, seasonal cycle* and the *micro cycle* (moon phase is usually best for past events).

4. **Identify any alignment within your cycle**

As shared with you in previous pages.

5. **Choose an oracle deck and pick a card**

You may have an intention or question about that moment of time, set that and then pull a card and place it on top of your Genius Wheel.

6. **Journal and reflect**

On what has come up on your Genius Wheel, how does this

reflect on the moment you picked? What does the alignment or lack of the alignment tell you? What energies were present and how do they relate to the challenge you've experienced? What new insight or understanding do you have? How can you use what you've learnt here to guide you forward?

7. **Compare Now with 7 Years Ago:**

   1. **Re-identify your current *macro cycle***

   BY NOW, I am sure you understand why the *macro cycle* is so important and always our starting point.

   2. **Reflect to 7 years ago from today**

   Reflect on either 2018, 2019, or 2020, consider the wins and opportunities or the challenges, and lessons that shaped your journey in life, business, health, and finances. Where were you thriving, and where did you feel stuck? What excited you, and what required growth? How was your macro cycle and the energy of it influencing you at that time.

   3. **Fast forward to now**

   Now, as you look at the year ahead (2025, 2026, and 2027) — what did you learn above that you can apply to now? What patterns do you recognise and what insights arise? How can you carry forward the wisdom from the past into now? How might your macro cycle support or show up for you? How have you grown or moved forward? What maturity, growth and genius have you galvanised? How can you be proud of yourself in terms of the last 7-year personal growth cycle?

8. **Chart your Course Forward:**

CHARTING our course forward enables us to trust the flow of things and to connect with a future version of ourselves, one who is wiser than we are right now. What a gift!

. . .

THE ONLY THING any of us should be ever chasing is the next version of ourselves and by using The Genius Wheel®, we can do so. Below I will share with you a variety of different ways you can chart your course forward. This will be very similar to the action we took in number 6, charting your course back but instead we are charting forward.

STEPS:

1. **Pick a significant moment in the near future (within the next 2 to 3 years)**

Your significant moment could be a month from now, a year or maybe up to 3 years but don't pick further ahead than that. Perhaps you have a big event coming up, something you'd like to launch or a career move you'd like to make? Maybe you are considering having a medical procedure or moving abroad? Make sure the date is of significance to you in terms of leveraging an opportunity and that you have a question around it.

2. **Write down the date**

Write the date of your significant event onto a piece of paper — if you want to add your micro cycle, you'll need an exact date but otherwise the month and year is enough.

3. **Create your Genius Wheel**

CREATE your Genius Wheel including your *macro cycle, seasonal cycle* and *micro cycle* where possible. Please note your *macro* and *seasonal cycle* is the most important if you are looking ahead in the future and it's best to add the moon phase (as oppposed to your menstrual cycle) for the *micro cycle* unless you are looking within a month or so ahead.

4. Identify any alignment within your cycle

As shared with you above. Here you might want to shift or change the date to find alignment. What would happen if you pushed it forward a few months or back? Play around here to see what's possible.

5. Choose an oracle deck and pick a card

Remind yourself of an intention or question you have about this significant date and then pull a card and place it on top of your Genius Wheel.

6. Journal and reflect

Reflect on what has come up on your Genius Wheel, how does this reflect on the moment you picked? What does the alignment or lack of the alignment tell you? What energies will be present and how do they relate to the opportunity you'd like to leverage? What new insight or understanding do you have? How can you use what you've learnt here to guide you forward?

9. Create the Map for your 7-Year Cycle:

ANOTHER POWERFUL WAY TO chart your course forward is by creating your own personal Genius Wheel for the next 7 years as a wheel! I have shared our case study Jo's Genius Wheel on the next page.

The Genius Wheel

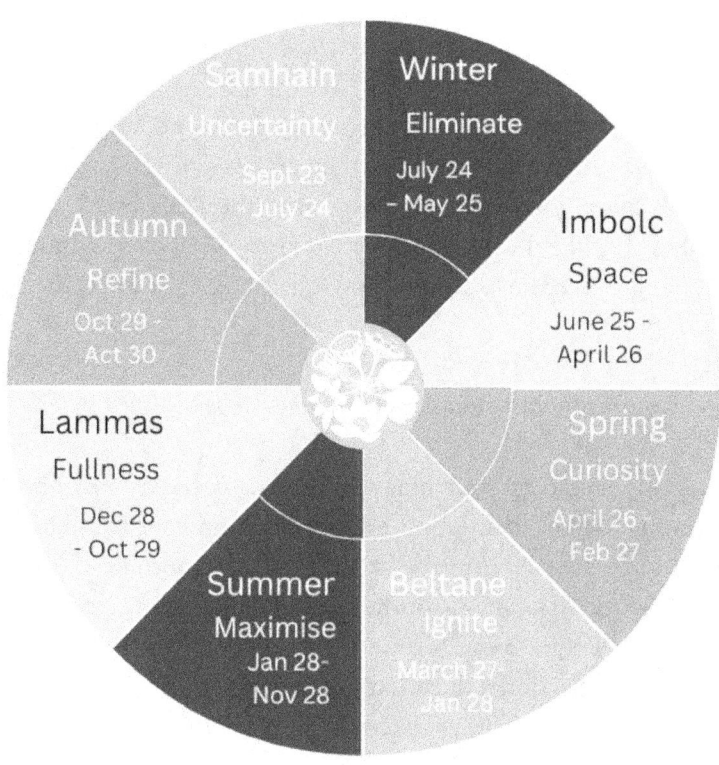

Image D

STEPS:

1. Download your editable 7-year Genius Wheel

You can find your downloadable and fillable PDF wheel at Substack.

2. Identify your current *macro cycle*

REMIND yourself of your current *macro cycle* and importantly the dates of it as in the table you created in Chapter 7. Once you have done this insert your current season into the PDF, by logging your dates into the wheel i.e. if your current season is *winter* (elimination), add the dates like the example shown in *Image D* above (July 2024 to May 2025).

3. Complete the wheel in clockwise order

Start by ensuring your macro season is correctly positioned on the Genius Wheel, beginning at 12 o'clock and moving clockwise: *winter* (north), *Imbolc* (northeast), *spring* (east), *Beltane* (southeast), *summer* (south), *Lammas* (southwest), *autumn* (west), and *Samhain* (northwest). Then, move around the wheel in clockwise order, assigning each section a duration of 10.5 months. If we continue with the example above, *Imbolc* (space) is next, meaning you would label the dates as June 2025 to April 2026. Continue adding dates in this way around the wheel. Keep in mind that the 0.5-month increments can make things a bit tricky, but just do a rough first draft, then adjust a few of the dates by about a month to ensure your full 7-year cycle ends in the correct place.

10. Align your Vision with your Genius Wheel:

BY PRACTISING ALL the above steps, you will become more intimate with your personal growth cycle and build trust with it. You may find many more creative ways to use your Genius Wheel and I'd love you to share them with me and the community in Substack. But I'd love to share one final way with you and that is by aligning your future vision with your Genius Wheel. I've outlined the steps for you below.

AS A REMINDER the only thing any of us should be chasing is the future version of ourselves and it's at this stage, we are really going to connect with her. You will need at least 30 minutes for this exercise and I invite you to go somewhere special, perhaps a trip to the beach with your journal or find a comfortable spot in your favourite chair, light a candle and some chilled vibes in the background.

STEPS:

1. **Pause and reflect**

Once you've arrived in your chosen space, take a moment to pause and reflect on who is the version of you that you'd like to become in 7 years time — 2031, 2032 or 2033. Write down the year in your journal.

2. **Identify your macro season**

Remind yourself of what macro season you'll be in — it will be the same as now. Make a note of it and the energy it carries.

3. **Close your eyes**

TO CONNECT with that version of yourself. Place a hand on your heart and take a few conscious breaths. Invite this version of you into your space. Then start a sentence, it's 2031 and I'm so happy and grateful...

Write down what you have achieved in the past 7 years. How are you feeling? What have you learnt and overcome? What are your wins and what are you celebrating? How did you get there? What happened along the way? Who have you become? What impact have you made?

AS I HAVE MENTIONED PREVIOUSLY, it is highly normal for people to feel anxious about their *winter* phase. I myself have felt the same but we have to trust with all literal and metaphorical deaths we experience, rebirth is a part of that process. With it we bring greater wisdom, maturity and growth to all that we do. We may worry about losing someone, struggling with finances or going into menopause but my hope is that The Genius Wheel® will help you to leverage all of these phases and become all that you are meant to be.

NOW YOU HAVE your 7-year personal growth cycle and The Genius Wheel® framework, to act as a map and guide to orientate yourself. You've created a vision of all you have achieved within this next cycle, and I look forward to seeing how this unfolds for you.

TELL me more about your unique personal growth cycle in either the Substack community and/or book a Coaching Intensive with me, where we can map your personal 7-year timeline together.

I HAVE SHARED ANCIENT IDEAS, along with yogic and shamanic traditions, in this book. What I present here is a collation of these wisdoms as my mind and body have understood, processed and integrated them — offered to you through my own lived experience and interpretation.

BEFORE WE DEPART, here is a poem from my dear friend and retreat co-host during the Covid era:

It's not your time by Gemma Williams[5]

"I want to curl up in a ball and bury my body into the earth,
But she whispered, "it's not your time".
I want to hide deep in the forest so no one can find me.
But she whispered, "it's not your time"
I want to cover myself with leaves and dive deep into the ocean.
But she whispered, "it's not your time"
I want to hide in the caves on mountain tops and walk beyond the desert.
But she whispered, "it's not your time"

She whispered...

I grew you from the earth so you could have roots and stand tall.
I made you from the stars so you could shine bright.
I made you from the rivers so you could flow with all of life.
I made you from the riverbeds so you could find your way.
I made you from the winds so you could fly.
I made you from the fires so your desires and passions can burn.

I made you, my child, to enjoy all of me. Your life is a gift, a prayer of life.
From me to you.

---

5. Poem and accompanying image by Gemma Williams. All rights reserved. Yoga Teacher Training https://gemyoga.co.uk/

**Please honour this gift and nurture your gifts.
And one day it will be time."**

FROM ME TO YOU
PLEASE HONOUR THIS GIFT AND NURTURE YOUR GIFTS

About the Author:

As a coach I have been described as a 'soul archaeologist', someone who uncovers the deeper truths buried beneath the surface of what is shared. My clients often say I have an intuitive ability to see beyond what is presented — understanding what lies unspoken and recognising the core needs behind their expressed desires. By connecting the dots between patterns, motivations, and experiences, I help bring clarity to even the most complex challenges.

Through thoughtful dialogue and a deep sense of attunement, I guide my clients to shift their perspectives, opening the door to new possibilities and greater self-awareness. I help them see their lives, decisions, and aspirations through a fresh lens — one that reflects their authentic values and untapped potential. This capacity to adjust and align with each individual's unique energy allows me to meet them where they are and gently lead them to where they truly want to be.

My approach is rooted in creating meaningful, transformative conversations. I don't offer quick fixes or temporary solutions. Instead, I work to help clients address the underlying blocks that keep them stuck, unlocking real and lasting change. By seeing the whole person and honouring the interconnectedness of their experiences, I empower my clients to achieve not just their goals but a more profound sense of purpose and alignment.

For those ready to dive deep and rediscover themselves, I provide a safe, intuitive, and supportive space for exploration and transformation — helping you reconnect with your true essence and chart a path toward authentic fulfilment.

Connect with Me:

Ready to unlock your genius? Visit thegeniuswheel.com to learn more, or step into the heart of the community on Substack. When you join, you'll receive a powerful welcome pack filled with tools, insights, and guided resources — everything you need to begin activating your 7-year personal growth cycle and living in alignment with your true purpose.

LinkedIn: @luluminns
Instagram: @thegeniuswheel
She Rebel Radio Podcast®: @sherebelradio

xo, Lulu

NOTES

ACKNOWLEDGMENTS

I'd love to start by expressing my deepest gratitude to everyone who has supported *She Rebel Radio*® over the years — my clients, listeners, sponsors and to all the women who have ever attended a retreat with me. Both the podcast and my work with women have been, in many ways, an unexpected study in what truly fulfils us, connects us, and aligns us with *our* path — not someone else's.

In a world where the internet encourages too many carbon copies, my clients and guests have been on unique journeys — ones I'm always committed to honouring.

A huge thank you to my sister, Cara Minns Johnson, for pouring her heart and soul into designing the book's cover. As a mother of two (ages 5 and 7), finding the time wasn't easy, but I loved seeing you return to your artistic genius (yes genius) whilst navigating your 8th personal growth cycle. I'll never forget the days of childhood when you bossed me around with your alter ego, Miss Billings, who once told me the shading on my vase was all wrong — I was only 4! Haha! Lots of love, sis.

A heartfelt thank you to our case study, Jo Myles. I first saw Jo speak at Clare Griffiths' Thrive brunches, which I've barely missed in the last 7 years. When considering a case study, I felt an intuitive nudge to 'stalk' you online and see if I could write about your cycle. I did, and our conversation was amazingly aligned. You totally 'got it' and shared how the Wheel of the Year was integral to your own artistic work. Being in your *winter* phase was a particularly poignant time for me to share your 7-year personal growth cycle. Thank you for your unreserved support and for being so open with everything you shared (imagine if you had hated it!).

The work of Sharon Blackie, Alexandra Pope, and Sjanie Wurlitzer has been a constant source of inspiration to me. I will forever be grateful for your wisdom and will continue recommending your books to every woman I meet! I can only hope that those who read this book will feel called to recommend it so passionately.

Finally, I'd like to extend my gratitude to my Editor, Mary-Rose Lobo, and Copy Editor, Gillian Pawley. Your steadfast support and deep understanding of the book's essence, whilst honouring my voice, have been invaluable.

∼

Appendix A

Jo Myles: A journey of Growth and Creative Evolution

In 2000, at the age of 22, Jo Myles had already completed her degree in textiles and was on the brink of entering her 4th personal growth cycle. As a student, she secured an internship with the renowned fashion designer, Alexander McQueen, marking the early stages of her career.

Jo's role grew quickly, and she soon found herself coordinating McQueen's prestigious catwalk shows. She was involved in the entire process, from turning initial sketches into real outfits to overseeing fittings and managing archives. Despite her young age, Jo was already managing a team of interns, displaying early signs of her leadership and creative flair.

Jo's personal development was mirrored by the phases of her growth cycle. When she began working with McQueen, she was in the *spring* phase of her 4th cycle (June 1998 to April 1999), a time of renewal and new beginnings. This energy carried her into the *Beltane* phase, igniting her passion for fashion, management and the creative arts.

In 2002, Jo transitioned into a new role as a buyer for the high-street fashion brand, Laura Ashley. This shift coincided with the *autumn* part of her personal growth cycle, a period of refining and solidifying her career path. However, by 2004, during her *winter* phase, Jo left Laura Ashley to focus on a similar role at Warehouse. This phase also brought a growing dissatisfaction with the fast fashion industry, particularly its lack of sustainability and poor working conditions. Jo's disillusionment planted a seed of change — she realised she wanted to disrupt the industry and forge her own path.

In 2007, at just 28 years old and entering the *Beltane* phase of her 5th growth cycle, Jo took a bold step and started her own business from her kitchen table. Armed with only £5,000 in savings (about £10,000 today), she began crafting unique, personal gifts whilst balancing the demands of starting a family. Her creative spark and determination paid off — within just 16 months, she became one of the top-grossing partners on Not On The High Street.

By 2011, Jo's business had flourished, and she was ready to incorporate her small venture into a formal company, which she named *3 Blonde Bears*, inspired by her 3 children. This transition occurred during the *Imbolc* phase of her growth cycle, a time for fresh starts and new ventures. With her business officially established, Jo's creativity continued to thrive.

Between 2012 and 2014, *3 Blonde Bears Ltd* expanded into a team of 35 employees. Jo, now 35 and in the midst of her 6th personal growth cycle, relished her role as the creative leader of her team whilst also cherishing moments with her family. With a customer base of over

17,000, she had an intuitive connection to the needs of mothers and children. Her company earned multiple awards, including the prestigious 2012 *Partner of the Year* award from *Not On The High Street*, and saw remarkable financial growth, with a predicted turnover increase of 50%. During this time, *3 Blonde Bears* was also recognised as one of the most creatively disruptive companies in the Startups 100 list for 3 consecutive years (2012–2014). These achievements occurred during her *spring, Beltane,* and *summer* phases, a period of approximately 32 months (10.5 months in each phase) marked by creativity, innovation, and the flourishing of her ideas alongside her small but expanding team.

However, in 2017, Jo experienced a turning point. A cancer diagnosis caused her to reflect deeply on both her life and work-life balance. This period marked the *winter* phase of her 6th personal growth cycle, a time often associated with elimination. In July 2018, Jo made the difficult decision to close *3 Blonde Bears*, signalling the end of a significant chapter in her journey. Whilst the *winter* phase can feel like a time of loss, it is also an opportunity for transformation and renewal, paving the way for the next cycle of growth — an invitation to re-root ourselves within a deeper truth.

Jo was already on a path of transformation, rediscovering her creative roots and embracing her role as a full-time maker and artist. As she prepared to enter the *Imbolc* phase of her 7th personal growth cycle, she felt ready to step more fully into this new chapter of her life. However, during this time of renewal, her relationship with her husband, and father of her children, began to unravel. Despite the emotional challenges, reconnecting with her creativity became a source of strength for Jo. It allowed her to re-root herself in a deeper truth, aligning her life more authentically with her artistic passion and personal values.

By 2021, at 42 years old, Jo was thriving in her 7th personal growth cycle, fully immersed in the vibrant *summer* phase of her journey. She had established herself as a successful independent international artist and maker, with her work featured on *Sky Arts* that year, and shortlisted for the prestigious *Glyndebourne Tour Art Competition*. In November of 2021, Jo co-founded *The Sussex Contemporary Ltd*, a platform designed to uplift and support Sussex-linked artists. As the creative director, her mission was clear: to share the knowledge, passion, and lessons she had garnered over two decades in the creative industries, whilst creating a supportive community for fellow Sussex artists.

In 2022, as she transitioned into the *Lammas* phase of her growth cycle, Joanna was able to celebrate the richness of her achievements. Her artwork was exhibited in *The Turner Contemporary Open*, and she was elected as director trustee of the *Ditchling Museum of Art + Craft* — both affirmations of her growing influence in the art world. Personally, her life had expanded too, as she found love again and embraced her new role as a mother of 5, blending her family with her partner's 2 children.

However, in 2024 when she hit the *Samhain* phase of her cycle, her relationship became something that felt less certain. Jo undertook some deep trauma work and set an intention for the year of truth. And boy, did that intention deliver as she found herself needing to challenge some bad behaviour of others both in business and in her relationships. It was a challenge for her to trust herself in these moments too. But in August 2024, after business matters had resolved she ended her relationship which had begun to wane, during her *autumn* phase in 2023. Being too busy to attend to it and putting everyone's needs before her own — she had tried to refine things but as she entered her *winter* phase, she ended the relationship. She said it felt like a sudden shift but in reality it had been building.

Looking at her alignment chart (in Chapter 10) — Jo entered *winter* (macro cycle) in July 2024 and the energy of *winter* (elimination). The seasonal cycle was *Lammas* (1st August to 21st September) which is fullness, but fullness can also mean 'enough' in this case representing the fullness or overload of the relationship into 'I've had enough'. The moon (micro cycle) was waning crescent for 5 days, (representing *Samhain* and *uncertainty*) going into the new moon and *elimination* on the 2nd September. Jo said she did feel *uncertain* and began to doubt herself, needing to remind herself she had made the decision to end the relationship. And if she'd had her Genius Wheel, it would have helped her to understand the energies within her cycle. Pulling an oracle card for her, the card represented shape-shifting and transformation, and an immersion into water.

Jo shared how poignant our conversation was in January 2025, at the point of her relationship breakdown, she and I had not yet connected about the drafting of her case study for this book.

From *August to September* as the seasons waned into *winter*, Jo also descended into her macro season of *winter*. She has said she had to 'dig deep and leverage herself' (her genius) to replace a lost salary within the household. Intuitively she decided she would cut out alcohol and drink lots of water. She prioritised work events and not social ones which she did not have the capacity for. She also cancelled the call she and I had scheduled. Jo needed to attend the bare bones of life - her children, her work and herself. Two of her cats even disappeared but returned at the start of the year. So she rested with her animals, and gave herself a luxurious spa membership for the year which as she will be moving into the *Imbolc* phase of her macro cycle later in the year, the *space* for self nurture, is perfect.

I asked her what she hoped for within her 8th personal growth cycle, and she said: "*A new home in a place that connects with my soul. Growing The Sussex Contemporary community and outreach work within marginalised communities. Stepping into a national Chairship position within the arts, and to start an MA in Cultural Leadership.*"

Jo's innate genius clearly centres around creativity, bringing people together, and disrupting industries with foresight and innovation. Her journey has been one of transformation and resilience. The spark ignited during her time as an intern in her 4th growth cycle, working alongside a prolific fashion designer, set the tone for her career. She quickly learned to manage people, buy and sell, and navigate the fast-paced world of fashion. After enduring a challenging *winter* phase, she returned to her roots as a maker and creator, equipped with the lessons from her previous growth cycles — turning her experience and creativity into a driving force for her ongoing success.

- **1998–1999 (*spring* phase of 4th growth cycle):** Joanna begins her personal growth journey whilst working as an intern for Alexander McQueen, helping with catwalk shows, managing a team of interns, and overseeing outfit creations.
- **2000 (Age 21):** Joanna completes her textiles degree and continues to work with Alexander McQueen, gaining experience in fashion, management, and the creative arts.
- **2002 (*autumn* phase of 4th growth cycle):** Joanna transitions to a buyer role for Laura Ashley, refining her career in the fashion industry.
- **2004 (*winter* phase of 4th growth cycle):** Joanna leaves Laura Ashley and accepts a position at Warehouse. This period marks the beginning of her dissatisfaction with fast fashion, sparking her desire to disrupt the industry.
- **2007 (Age 28, *Beltane* phase of 5th growth cycle):** Joanna starts her own business from her kitchen table with £5,000 in savings, focusing on unique personal gifts and products. Within 16 months, she became one of the top-grossing partners on *Not On The High Street*.
- **2011 (*Imbolc* phase of 5th growth cycle):** Joanna incorporates her business into *3 Blonde Bears*, inspired by her 3 children, marking the formal establishment of her

company.
- **2012–2014 (*spring*, *Beltane*, and *summer* phases of 6th growth cycle):** *3 Blonde Bears Ltd* grows into a team of 35 people. Joanna's company wins multiple awards, including *Not On The High Street Partner of the Year* (2012) and is listed in the Startups 100 as one of the most creatively disruptive companies (2012–2014). The business sees significant financial growth during this period.
- **2017 (*winter* phase of 6th growth cycle):** A health issue prompts Joanna to reevaluate her life and work. She decides to close *3 Blonde Bears*, marking the end of this business chapter.
- **July 2018:** Joanna officially folds *3 Blonde Bears*, ending her *winter* phase and preparing for the next cycle of personal growth.
- **2021 (Age 42, *summer* phase of 7th growth cycle):** Joanna flourishes as an independent international artist and maker. Her work is featured on *Sky Arts*, and she is shortlisted for the *Glyndebourne Tour Art Competition*. In November 2021, she co-founds *The Sussex Contemporary Ltd*, a platform to support Sussex-linked artists. As creative director, she shares her two decades of experience in the creative industries with a wider community.
- **2022 (*Lammas* phase of 7th growth cycle):** Joanna's work is exhibited in *The Turner Contemporary Open*, and she is elected director trustee of the *Ditchling Museum of Art + Craft*. On a personal level, she finds love again and becomes a mother of 5, blending her family with her partner's 2 children.
- **2022 (*Samhain* and *winter* phase of 7th growth cycle):** Difficulties within relationships and deep trauma work connecting her to truth.

Jo Myles' story is one of evolution, creativity and resilience. Her journey through the phases of personal growth has seen her rise in the fashion industry, navigate the challenges of entrepreneurship, and ultimately embrace change, all whilst staying true to her passion for disrupting the creative landscape.

Appendix B
Understanding each phase

SAMHAIN 9PM NORTH WEST WATER/EARTH SOUL STAR WANING CRESCENT	**WINTER SOLSTICE** MIDNIGHT NORTH EARTH ROOT - I AM NEW MOON
IMBOLC 3AM NORTH EAST EARTH/AIR SACRAL - I FEEL WAXING CRESENT	**SPRING EQUINOX** 6AM EAST AIR SOLAR PLEXUS - I DO 1ST QUARTER
BELTANE 9AM SOUTH EAST AIR/FIRE HEART - I LOVE WAXING GIBBOUS	**SUMMER SOLSTICE** MIDDAY SOUTH FIRE THROAT - I SPEAK FULL
LAMMAS 3PM SOUTH WEST FIRE/WATER THIRD EYE - I SEE WANING GIBBOUS	**AUTUMN EQUINOX** 6PM WEST WATER CROWN - I UNDERSTAND 2ND QUARTER

www.ingramcontent.com/pod-product-compliance
Lightning Source LLC
Chambersburg PA
CBHW071201070526
44584CB00019B/2882